D0327357

# THE STRANGE CASE OF
# THOMAS WALKER

THOMAS WALKER
*by Romney*

# THE STRANGE CASE
# OF THOMAS WALKER

## Ten Years in the Life
## of a Manchester Radical

by

FRIDA KNIGHT

With a Foreword by
G. D. H. COLE

1957
LAWRENCE & WISHART LTD.
LONDON

*Printed in Great Britain by*
*The Camelot Press Ltd., London and Southampton*

# FOREWORD

## *By* G. D. H. Cole

THE story of the repression in Great Britain during the years that followed the great French Revolution of 1789 has been told by a number of authors and from a number of different angles of vision. Best known of these studies are Philip A. Brown's *The French Revolution in English History*—an excellent work—and Mr. and Mrs. Hammond's classic account in *The Town Labourer.*

What has not been done at all adequately hitherto is the telling of the story in relation to particular persons and places outside London, though the Corresponding Society movement and Major Cartwright's Society for Constitutional Information had affiliates or related bodies in a large number of cities and industrial areas, and the prosecutions that were set on foot against them extended to many places outside London and Central Scotland.

The historical account still needs to be enlarged by a considerable amount of local research, especially in such places as Manchester, Sheffield, Norwich and Newcastle-on-Tyne, in all of which there are libraries containing a good deal of material that has not yet been adequately used.

Mrs. Knight's short study of Thomas Walker, the Manchester merchant, who took the lead among the Manchester Radicals during those critical years, fills in one of these gaps. Fortunately there is, in Walker's case, a fair amount of readily accessible material to work upon—the full report of the trial, in which Erskine was Walker's leading counsel for the defence, and Walker's own story of the events that led up to the trial. But apart from these Mrs. Knight has made good use of other sources—especially of the correspondence between the Walkers and the young James Watt, son of the inventor, who acted as Walker's business agent in Italy as well as being his confidant about current political affairs. The result is a vivid, as well as a scholarly, account of an interesting and attractive person who

has hitherto lacked a biographer and is recorded even in the
D.N.B. only indirectly, in a very short passage of the entry
dealing with his son, also Thomas Walker, best remembered as
the editor and author of that curious, short-lived journal *The
Original*. My only regret relating to Mrs. Knight's study is that
she has not been able to find more information about the
character and scale of Walker's business activities in the fustian
trade—for example, to what extent he was an actual master
manufacturer as well as a merchant, how many workers he
employed, how many of them worked on his premises and how
many at home, with what markets he dealt both at home and
abroad, and whether his business failure was due mainly to
ordinary commercial causes or to his political activities, which
clearly did have some part in it.

It would, however, be churlish to complain of Mrs. Knight
for failing to discover information that in all probability no
longer exists. It is much more to the point to congratulate her
on what she has been able to do, and to venture the hope that
her success will encourage other students of the social history
of the period to follow her excellent example.

*All Souls College,*
*Oxford.*
*July, 1956*

# AUTHOR'S ACKNOWLEDGEMENTS

MY interest in Thomas Walker was aroused when my husband, three years ago, happened on an eighteenth-century volume of collected pamphlets in a second-hand bookshop. The book contained the verbatim report of Walker's trial for sedition and conspiracy, and turned out to be the signed copy presented by the merchant to his defending counsel, Felix Vaughan. The story, exciting in itself and analogous to certain cases of our own day, stimulated me to set off on the search for the truth behind the trial.

The investigations took me far afield; as far indeed as Ballarat, New South Wales, whence Mr. John Curwen-Walker (great-great-grandson of Thomas) has given me useful clues, and Kenya, where Dr. Drury, another descendant, has valuable family relics. My acknowledgements and thanks are due to these descendants of the great Radical, but above all to Mr. Roger Dru Drury, of Snape, whose willingness to lend material on Walker's family life has been invaluable.

I must also thank many kind friends and advisers: Mr. Stanley Horrocks, chief Assistant Librarian at Manchester Central Library, and Miss Hilda Lofthouse, of Chetham's Library, for their patience and great helpfulness; Dr. Chaloner, Dr. Plumb, Mr. James Klugmann, Professor Asa Briggs, and Mr. Edward Thompson, for reading and criticising the manuscript; Mr. Eric Robinson and Professor Aspinall for indicating fruitful sources, and those in charge of the Search Room at the Public Record Office for their assistance in exploring those sources; the Treasury Solicitor for permission to reproduce documents in his files; the librarians of the Birmingham Library, of Nuffield College and of the Barlaston collection, for their help and advice; and those friends on whom I have inflicted myself during my travels, for their forbearance. Above all I must thank Professor G. D. H. Cole who encouraged me to start the search and Mr. Kingsley Martin who encouraged me to carry it on.

FRIDA KNIGHT

*November, 1956*

# CONTENTS

# LIST OF ILLUSTRATIONS

## CHAPTER I

# MANCHESTER (1780-1790)

## 1. WALKER'S FAMILY AND FRIENDS

DURING the summer of 1793, Thomas Walker, the Manchester cotton merchant and former Borough-reeve sat for his portrait to George Romney. The two men were friends, and Romney, painter *par excellence* of famous beauties, smart young aristocrats, leaders of fashion, and political celebrities, portrayed the provincial industrialist with far more depth and sympathy than the usual run of his subjects.

The picture, though now darkened by the dust and smoke of nearly two centuries, shows a strikingly good-looking and distinguished man, obviously someone of great character, strong convictions, and considerable means. One would think, a pillar of society.

And so indeed he was. Charles James Fox described him to the House of Commons as "worthy, from opulence and every other consideration, to be ranked with the best men in this house"; the Honourable Thomas Erskine, later Lord Chancellor, spoke of him as "a merchant of honour, property and respect, who has long enjoyed the friendship of many of the worthiest and most illustrious persons in the kingdom . . .".

Yet, at the very time Romney was painting him, Thomas Walker was under the shadow of arrest: he had been accused of being "a pernicious, wicked and ill-disposed person", of "uttering treason and sedition", of conspiring to overthrow the Constitution and to assist the enemies of his country—there had even been talk of high treason. A trial loomed ahead, in which, if enough evidence were presented, he might be sentenced to transportation, to imprisonment for life, possibly even to death.

How did this happen? Was there some fatal mistake? Was Walker a schizophrenic, a split personality, leading a double life? Was there evidence to justify the accusations? Was he a criminal, or was he the victim of a blunder, an accident, a plot? The answer to the enigma lies in the story of a decade in Walker's life—the years 1784 to 1794.

The story, however, begins on 3rd April, 1751, when Thomas was born in the manorial village of Manchester, a sizeable but as yet undeveloped community in the county of Lancashire.

His parents were well-to-do, cultured people. One can see from their portraits, painted by a pupil of Gainsborough, that they were a worthy, respectable couple, with plenty of character and good humour in their honest, likeable faces. Thomas senior, who claimed descent from an old Monmouthshire family, had started life in Bristol, but had removed to Manchester to continue his career as a merchant and build up a business there some time before the birth of his first son.

Very little is known about the elder Walkers; one curious scrap of information tells us that Thomas's mother was the first person to carry an umbrella in Manchester, and that she was mobbed for her pains! We can if we like deduce from this that it was from her that Thomas got his common sense, his obstinately progressive character and sturdy independence; while his shrewdness and flair for business came from his father. We have no clue as to where he got his sense of humour, his fighting spirit and his extraordinary generosity—the characteristics which were the cause of his downfall and also his salvation, and which are so vividly reflected in the Romney portrait.

Thomas Walker was born into a period of widespread social ferment—a period when primitive prejudices were being attacked more forcibly than ever before by the Rationalists, and superstition by the scientists of the new age of reason; when the privileges and power of the aristocracy were being challenged all over Europe by men who worked with hand and brain; and when ordinary people had, through the weekly newspapers and the better means of communication, easy access, for the first time in history, to news of national and international happenings.

Like other bright boys of his generation, Thomas read the Radical journals and the pamphlets that were circulating, and the writings of Rousseau, Voltaire, Locke, Hume; he followed the political controversies of the day; he looked about him and saw the crying social injustices, the poverty and hunger and ignorance of the people, ruled without any regard for their real needs by an unrepresentative Court clique. He came to know of the absurd electoral system—by which a seat in Parliament was ensured to the highest bidder, or to the most servile of George III's yes-men. He learned of the cruel and wasteful war waged in America against men who wanted only to manage their own affairs; and of the shocking state of things in France, reported by observant travellers and writers, such as Arthur Young.

There was enough food for thought to turn any intelligent lad brought up, as young Walker was, by sensible parents in a broadminded Christian home, into a convinced Radical, if not a revolutionary.

Even after entering the family business Thomas kept up his intellectual activities, reading a great deal, and regularly attending the meetings of the Literary and Philosophical Society. It was there that he met his best friends—Dr. Ferriar, one of the chief physicians at the local Infirmary, who was an excellent doctor with advanced ideas; Joseph Collier, the surgeon; Samuel Jackson, a progressive cotton merchant like himself; Thomas Cooper, brilliant lawyer and research chemist in a local bleachers' firm—a dynamic personality whose bitingly witty pen was constantly in action against obscurantism and reaction.

Thomas Walker was influenced by these friends and by his reading, but most of all, of course, by the realities of the time. At the Walkers' very doorstep the Industrial Revolution was coming to life, and social upheaval and technical change were manifest on every side. Lancashire had become the centre of progress; its cotton industry was developing by leaps and bounds, its inventors creating machines which increased the possibilities of production a hundredfold, and in turn led to new inventions and further technical and economic advances.

Outside the industrial areas the importance of these advances was recognised by many Whigs and Radicals, and by scientific societies, who honoured the inventors with their praise, with medals and grants, and efforts to break down the unsatisfactory existing system of patents.

The manufacturers of Lancashire also appreciated and encouraged new ideas and discoveries; they were on the whole an energetic and enterprising lot, men who spotted their opportunities, seized them and made the most of them.

It was the aristocratic landed gentry of the ruling class who did not appreciate the trend of things; they sensed that a new class was rising and threatening to supersede them. The heirs of ancient families, and the more recent arrivals to the nobility (who had reached court circles and ministries through their pockets), realised that the industrialists had come to stay; and though it was clear that there was elbow room for both sections of society, and that live and let live was the only possible policy for them, they did not—and could hardly be expected to—love these ambitious, hard-headed northern business men, most of them self-made rather than inheritors of estates, tough types who were familiar with their workmen and called a spade a spade, in broad Lancashire or Yorkshire dialect.

Although Walker differed from other industrialists in being neither self-made nor a native of Lancashire, he was of course entirely on their side; and it made him very indignant to see how the manufacturing communities were despised and cold-shouldered, their importance ignored or disregarded by the ministries of North and Pitt. He and his friends were even more irritated by the fact that the citizens of Manchester were not represented in any way in the House of Commons.

It was possible for those who boasted some social standing to get their grievances aired, very occasionally, in Parliament through their personal contacts with Whig members of other towns, or Whig peers. Walker, for instance, as his fortune and influence increased, was able to bring the interests of his community to the fore through his friends Lord Derby, Grey and Fox. But he realised that this was a most unsatisfactory way of proceeding, and saw that while the well-to-do could sometimes advance their cases, the vast majority of the town's population had no means whatever of voicing their needs and troubles. And it was this realisation that first brought him into the movement for electoral reform—a connection which was later to cost him so dear.

However, at the time when he was beginning to take a

THOMAS WALKER, SENIOR
*School of Gainsborough*

MARKET STREET, MANCHESTER

practical interest in these things, the early campaign for reform led by Major John Cartwright and Christopher Wyvill was dying out, and the later one was not yet born.

In the early 1780s he had his hands full with other things. He had grown up and learned his trade and taken over his father's firm, in partnership with his younger brother Richard. Together they established the business on a sounder basis than ever before, expanded their connections at home and abroad, brought themselves up to date with the latest inventions and equipment.

Thomas Walker was kept well informed on technical developments by Matthew Boulton, with whom he was on the best of terms. Boulton was at this time well known as the leading producer of modern machinery, in co-operation with James Watt, at the Soho works in Birmingham. He and Walker had much in common, and their friendship was more than good business relations; both were enterprising industrialists, but they were men of a certain vision and of humanist ideals as well, and they honestly believed that their advances in industry were for the benefit of mankind as well as themselves. They shared a keen interest outside business, in philosophy, politics, literature and science.

Walker also greatly admired James Watt; and when Watt's son, James junior, came to Manchester for a commercial apprenticeship the Walkers welcomed him into their family circle. Young James was good-looking, well-educated (his father had sent him to study science and languages in Switzerland and Germany), and an enthusiastic Radical; he became deeply attached to the Walkers, who considered him almost a son, and eventually gave him a highly confidential post in their firm—travelling as their agent in Europe in 1792 and 1793.

But as early as 1782 Walker was in touch with Soho, doing his best to help Boulton and Watt by making their engines known and sold in Manchester. He wrote many letters to Boulton, addressing him as his dear friend, and introducing possible customers; among others he sent Count Soderini the Venetian minister to visit Soho in 1787.

He was responsible too for introducing Thomas Cooper, his fellow member of the Literary and Philosophical Society, to

Boulton and Watt. This resulted in a lifelong friendship between Cooper and young James, who, unlike his cautious father, was greatly attracted to revolutionary ideas, and became Cooper's inseparable companion in Manchester. A correspondence which started with a polite note on the subject of an engine ordered for a pump by Cooper's bleaching firm, continued off and on for many years—letters eventually going from Cooper in Philadelphia to young Watt in Naples and Leghorn. But before they became close friends Cooper's letters were mainly to Watt senior, and dealt with problems of furnaces, installations ("We are anxious to be on a right general plan in the outset, so that when the engine is once erected it may not become a perpetual Eyesore to us in the future"), smoke prevention, and so on; letters were accompanied by plans and diagrams on Cooper's side, while Watt sounded the chemist "about the best way of making *muriate exigue*, as I have undertaken to make it for Dr. Priestley".[1]

But to return to Thomas Walker. As a result of his resourcefulness, ability and energy, he was extremely successful. By 1784, when only thirty-four years old, he had come to be recognised as one of the leading men of the town, and was always being called on to act as committee member, or delegate, or sponsor for various public organisations. His support was sought and his signature asked for all sorts of causes and appeals. And as the manufacturers grew in importance and influence, Walker, as one of their leaders, became a figure of almost national importance and influence too.

Between 1780 and 1790 he was certainly to be envied: he was at the top of the tree, well off, with many interests, and a happy home life. He was married to a beautiful and intelligent woman (Hannah Shore Nightingale) and had six fine healthy children whom he adored. The family lived, during the summer, very comfortably in a big country house at Barlow, some five miles from the town, rented from Mr. Egerton, Member of Parliament for Newcastle-under-Lyme; Walker also had a winter residence and warehouse for business purposes, on South Parade in Manchester.

We are told that the Walker children—three boys and three

[1] Boulton-Watt Correspondence, 1786.

girls—"were all remarkable for great personal beauty and created a sensation when they drove into Manchester in the family carriage drawn by four horses, or when they appeared at the theatre".[1]

Walker's happiness would probably have been complete, had it not been for his tiresome social conscience, which marred his enjoyment of his large share of worldly goods; he consoled himself with the thought that reform would sooner or later come in England, and with it a good life for all and sundry. And he appeased his conscience by working to hasten the day.

It is strange that his fortune and position should not have affected his democratic outlook; but he became more rather than less of a Radical, and was always on equally good terms with his work-people, who regarded him as a personal friend, and with men like Matthew Boulton and the twelfth Lord Derby. Nor did being an important public figure spoil his sense of humour, to judge by certain stories about him; there is one which tells how, coming home from a political meeting one night, he noticed a man putting his head to the iron grating of a cellar window, and saying "Twig!", in answer to which a hand emerged, full of good things to eat. A few nights later Walker was passing the same cellar window, and thought he'd try his luck: he put his mouth to the grating, called out "Twig!" and waited a moment. A huge turkey leg was thrust out, which he grabbed and carried home in triumph to his astonished family.[2]

Another story which indicates that Walker liked a good laugh, is a letter sent to him in the form of a "memorial" by two friends, who needed some cloth of his manufacture for themselves and their furniture. One "memorialist" explains that he "is touched by Distresses that go to the very Bottom of his Comforts . . . and contemplates with melancholy concern the forlorn and desolate Situation of his Chairs and Sopha without a decent covering to rescue them from absolute Nakedness". The other "anticipates with dismal Apprehensions the coming Horrors of approaching Winter through the ruins of dilapidated Waistcoats and lacerated Manchester". The writers "engage to pay the carriage of the several Parcels" and "solemnly declare

---

[1] Blanchard Jerrold. *The Original*, Preface, p. 119.     [2] Jerrold, op. cit., p. 43.

B

that neither their Upholsterers nor their Taylors Bills shall be transmitted to Mr. Walker"; and express their certainty that he will help them with spirit and enthusiasm, more especially when acquainted that "the Paper of the former's Apartments is French Grey, and the Coats of the Latter of British Blue".[1]

It is pretty certain that the memorialists got their cloth, for Walker's generosity was almost proverbial. He never failed to help anyone in need, or turned away from poverty or distress.

Wealth did not blind him to social injustice, but rather increased his awareness and horror of it. He made himself heartily disliked in some quarters by his outspoken championship of causes in which he believed, and by his relentless condemnation of what he was convinced was wrong.

Between 1780 and 1800 it was tempting to look at the bright side of the early Industrial Revolution, and to ignore its wrongs and evils. Most of the leading men of Manchester followed the line of least resistance; but there were a handful, who set out to expose and destroy the social evils around them—and of these Thomas Walker was one of the foremost and most indefatigable.

[1] Jerrold, op cit., pp. 42-5.

## CHAPTER II

# MANCHESTER (1780-1790)

## 2. People and Politics

M ANCHESTER, as Walker knew it, was a huddle of half-timbered black and white houses, leaning across narrow cobbled streets and straddling round a few squares and churchyards at the centre. The main hub of activity was Market Square, where Harrop, the Tory owner and publisher of the *Manchester Mercury*, most important of the local newspapers, had his shop and posted up the latest intelligence from home and abroad. Almost next door to this was Matthew Falkner's printing house, where Radical pamphlets and journals were on sale; a stone's throw away, in the Shambles, was Shaw's Punch House, the most popular of the many public houses, where much commercial and political business was done over brews of brandy and punch.

Walker's house was not many minutes from the town centre, in a quiet street looking on to St. Anne's churchyard. A few years earlier the house would have been almost on the edge of the town; but in the last quarter of the century Manchester had started the great spread—putting out street-tentacles of low brick dwellings interspersed with grim prisonlike mills and warehouses into the countryside around.

The Directory for 1794 tells us that Manchester "was accounted a large populous town even fifty years ago; but since that time it is supposed to have increased in more than a triple proportion both in respect to buildings and inhabitants.

"The houses amount to a number not far short of 12,000; and perhaps it may not be an over-rate to reckon seven persons to each . . . for though many hundred houses have been built in the course of a few late years, yet are they constantly engaged as soon as possible, the avidity for building increasing with every new accession of inhabitants, and rents rising to a degree scarcely known in other places . . . a guinea per square yard, chief rent, having been refused for some central plots."

Thus it appears that landowners and lawyers shared with the manufacturers the growing prosperity of the town. The Directory account goes on:

"The manufactures of this neighbourhood, from humble domestic beginnings, but two centuries ago, have now, after progressive improvements, acquired such celebrity, both in the scale of ornament and utility as to spread in ten thousand forms and colour not only in these kingdoms, but all over Europe and even into distant continents; being at once, most precious mines of well-earned private wealth, and sources of important contribution to the necessary public treasure of the state. Its post-office alone may afford an evidence of its extensive commerce."

The writer believes that 200,000 men, women and children are employed in the cotton factories "in the mere branches of preparing *warp* and *weft*. If to these be added the many hands applied to weaving etc. etc. etc. besides all the more general mechanics, as well as householders, domestic servants, etc. Manchester may be ranked as the most populous market-town in Great Britain." 68,580 inhabitants "is thought to be much under the sum of an actual enumeration".

The chief reason, of course, was the comparatively high wage rates and plentiful employment in the rising industry. "The advance of wages," wrote the Board of Agriculture's Lancashire reporter, "and the preference given to the manufacturing employment by the laborers in general, have induced many to forsake the spade for the shuttle"; champions of the agrarian employers complained of "the influx of wealth amongst the labouring class of Lancashire leading them into extravagant habits" such as "to indulge upon many occasions with the wheaten loaf"; fears were also expressed that the high wages would lead to the "corruption of the workmen in their moral and civil dispositions" and to "the disruption of the internal peace of the realm".[1]

But complaints did not stem the flood. Multitudes left the countryside and surged into the industrial area hoping to find,

[1] Witt Bowden, *Industrial Society in England towards the end of the 18th Century*, p. 253.

if not wealth, at least comparatively well-paid work. They came from the expropriated farms, the enclosed commons, the bankrupt shops, the ruined small "manufactories" of rural England, Wales, Ireland and the Scottish highlands. The arrival of one typical contingent is described in the *Manchester Mercury* of 24th May, 1785: "Last week, between forty and fifty North Britons with Bagpipes and other Music playing, arrived at Cromford, near Matlock, from Perth. They were immediately taken into the Service of Mr. Richard Arkwright. They appeared highly pleased with the reception and had a Dance in the Evening to congratulate each other on the performance of so long a Journey."

It was Josiah Wedgwood's boast that the potteries and other factories had transformed a crude, poverty-stricken district into a populous and prosperous one, with "the workmen earning near double their former wages—their houses mostly new and comfortable and the lands, roads, and every other circumstance, bearing evident marks of the most pleasing and rapid improvements".[1]

But there was another side to this pleasant picture of industrial prosperity, at any rate in Manchester: the evils of overcrowding, lack of hygiene, disease—some of the things that Thomas Walker wanted to fight. A contemporary observer wrote that "as Manchester may bear comparison with the metropolis itself in the rapidity with which whole new streets have been raised, and in its extension on every side towards the surrounding country: so it unfortunately vies with, or exceeds, the metropolis, in the closeness with which the poor are crowded in offensive, dark, damp and incommodious habitations, a too fertile source of disease".[2]

Walker's friend, Dr. Ferriar, one of the head doctors at the Infirmary, wrote in 1795 about the shocking housing conditions: "I have known several industrious families lost to the community by a short residence in damp cellars"; and "in a house in Bottle Street, most of the inhabitants are paralytic, in consequence of their situation in a blind alley which excludes them

---

[1] Witt Bowden, *Industrial Society in England towards the end of the 18th Century*, p. 255.

[2] Brockbank, *Portrait of a Hospital*, p. 37.

from light and air. Consumptions, distortion and idiocy are common in such recesses." The shortage of accommodation for the constant influx of would-be industrial workers was acute, and the doctor quoted as typical of the position in the available lodging-houses a case of "nine patients confined with fevers at the same time in one of these houses, crammed in three small dirty rooms . . .".[1]

That fevers and other diseases were rampant is not surprising, for in the 1780s there was no cleaning of the streets, and the drainage system (like the lighting) was practically non-existent. Among many of the "public nuisances" of that time, which contributed to the spread of disease, were "the laying of timber, dung and other things in the public streets", the "great number of uncovered cellar holes about the town", and "the suffering of swine to stray about the streets, which is not only a filthy but often a dangerous nuisance . . .".[2]

One "nuisance" (from which even modern inhabitants of Manchester still suffer in more or less degree) was the dust and smoke which defiled air and property as a result of the new factory chimneys. Thomas Cooper complained in a letter to young James Watt (22nd January, 1790) of "the smoke and dirt which now fall upon our white cloth and compel much additional and otherwise unnecessary Labour . . .". Elsewhere, while discussing Watt's smoke-consuming fireplaces, he observed that "though a man may not care for smoke himself, his neighbours will, and he may be induced to oblige them when no other inducement will prevail; and I think it is a question . . . whether smoking fire engines in or near a Neighbourhood do not legally amount to a Nuisance".

Short of installing Watt's fireplaces in all industrial premises, there was no satisfactory way of abolishing this particular nuisance. But the other causes of annoyance mentioned were in fact more or less controlled by the municipal authority of the time, the centuries-old "manorial court". This was headed by the Boroughreeve, or chief citizen (appointed by the Manor, every year presumably at the advice of leading persons of the town, for the Lord of the Manor, one of the Moseley family,

[1] Brockbank, *Portrait of a Hospital*, p. 38.
[2] Charge to the Court Leet, 1788.

took no active part in Manchester's affairs, apart from drawing his rents).

When Thomas Walker held the office of Boroughreeve, in 1790, he found himself responsible for law and order, with two chief constables and a squad of special police to assist him. He presided over a "jury" of twelve respectable citizens, elected, like himself, to take charge of the organisation and welfare of the town. Particular officers of the jury were detailed to deal with one or more "nuisances".

This was a very inadequate administration for such an important and rapidly growing town, and some more powerful and efficient body was obviously needed to cope with over-crowding, bad drainage, disease, drunkenness and other social evils—but party feeling was so strong that no reform was possible: the Tories who held the key positions were too much afraid that any change in local government structure would play into the hands of their adversaries.

The unusually bitter enmity of "High Church" Tories was largely due to the fact that Manchester had become the most important provincial centre of nonconformism—this could be traced back to the years when Protestant refugees from Europe settled in Lancashire and introduced their cotton weaving to these parts. However this may be, the dissenters were a power-ful force in the town; many of the leading manufacturers and merchants were dissenters, most of them were dissenters and Whigs as well, and so the objects of the Tories' political hostility, commercial jealousy and religious prejudice—a mixture pro-ductive of a fine brand of hatred.

Thomas Walker was one of the chief candidates for their detestation, being one of a small but active group of extremely radical Whigs; he was himself no dissenter but brought up to worship in the Church of England by his very devout father and mother. There was a larger group of lukewarm Whigs, less active than Walker's, but willing to support him on issues of general concern. The local dissenters, whether Whig or non-political, were on the whole progressive individuals, and would follow Walker rather than the reactionaries on issues affecting civil liberties; they could not be counted on to take action on anything which did not concern their own interests, though the

Radicals hoped that they would support the right side at the right moment in a crisis.

In some small degree, the political position in Manchester resembled that in Westminster, where the Tory Court clique held the administrative posts, opposed by a strongly Radical opposition group (headed by Fox) with an unwieldy, unreliable Whig, but non-radical, tail.

Just as the Tories in London controlled the laws, and the civic, religious and political life of the land, the Tories in Manchester ruled the local roost as justices of the peace, churchwardens and officers of the Court Leet. But the Whigs were becoming more and more influential. It was Walker and his friends who planned and carried out advances in local welfare, built the hospital, agitated for parliamentary representation. They had brought the town fame and prosperity by their initiative, and many of the population recognised them as their best friends, and supported them against the Tories. They had the backing of the lower middle class and of the skilled workers and artisans, who were an important part of the Manchester public and in some industries had a primitive form of trade union organisation, and some political experience.

But there was a fair section of society in Manchester who neither knew nor cared who ran the town, and could be swayed by demagogy or unscrupulous methods to hinder and harm policies of advance. Many of the rapidly growing Manchester proletariat were at this time industrially unorganised, politically unconscious, and—through no fault of their own—ignorant and illiterate. They led a hand-to-mouth existence, housed under the most wretched conditions, toiling for long hours in mills and workshops, with sleep or drink as their only escape from a grim meaningless life. It was from their ranks that the army got its soldiers in the 1790s—by "pressing" defenceless labourers or weavers, in unlit streets on dark nights—and from them that the Tories at the same period recruited their bands of hoodlums with promises of pay and strong liquor, when rioting and mob rule was the order of the day and the object the destruction of Radicals and dissenters.

However, between 1780 and 1790 Manchester appeared a peaceable enough community. The press gang was not much in evidence and riots were hardly known. Workers, whatever their pay and their living conditions, were in jobs and could eat.

Tories had no immediate reason for concern; Whigs of different shades of opinion had no special cause for division. And they all lived together comparatively amicably—the hatchet buried, temporarily and not very deep, but at least out of sight—sinking their differences in the interests of the local prosperity which was so important to them all.

## CHAPTER III

# THE FUSTIAN AFFAIR (1784-1785)

THERE was just one short period in the 1780s when the smooth surface of Manchester's life was badly ruffled; it was caused by an unwise move by the government in London in 1784, and resulted in a trial of strength between young Pitt, the recently appointed Prime Minister, and the cotton men, led by Thomas Walker. All Lancashire was up in arms, its indignation and annoyance having been roused by a measure that Pitt had introduced, completely disregarding their interests and feelings—the imposition of a tax on dyed cotton and cotton mixtures (known as fustians). The Prime Minister thought he had found an easy way to raise some cash for his exchequer, grievously depleted by the American War and the costly wasteful government of several decades. He did not imagine he was stirring up such a hornet's nest about him, nor did he perhaps realise the hardship that the measure would bring to the cotton trade—for the inordinately heavy increases in the cost of the most popular and necessary materials, to producers and consumers alike, was more than the precarious economy of Lancashire could stand.

Pitt insisted that the tax be introduced; and in the process, many onerous regulations were imposed on the manufacturers: bleachers and dyers had to get licenses; the taxes were collected by special excise commissioners, to whom manufacturers were obliged to give detailed information about their utensils and methods; excise men might enter a plant day or night in search of such information, and any obstruction by the owner might land him with a fine of £200.

Selling goods marked in counterfeit incurred a penalty of £100 and two hours in the pillory. And the owner responsible for counterfeiting the exciseman's stamp could expect nothing less than the death penalty.[1]

1 Witt Bowden, op. cit., p. 170.

No wonder Walker and his friends resented this high-handed inquisitorial law, which, if broken, resulted in the harshest punishment, if kept, resulted in near or complete ruin.

The authorities found few to defend the tax, although an anonymous correspondent wrote in the *Manchester Mercury* of 8th September, 1784, excusing it on the grounds that "an unfortunate war has caused such an expenditure of Wealth as calls for an immensity of Taxes to defray the Interest of the Sums borrowed".

The writer added that it was a misrepresentation to say that "Excise Officers may enter Private Houses in the night . . . the Entry cannot be made without their being accompanied by a constable; they are *not* accustomed to enter Bedchambers, to search into beds, drawers or desks, or to disturb the Repose of private Families. . . .".

This did not however appease the industrialists, who were already busy agitating for the repeal of the tax. Thomas Walker was one of the leaders from the start of the campaign, helping to form a committee which appealed for funds—it was announced on 27th August that "the MEMORIAL against the intended TAXES of 1d and 2d per yard on the FUSTIAN articles" would be "left for signing at H. Harrops' shop". Four days later a list appeared of three hundred and fifty subscribers whose donations made it possible to carry on effective agitation, by meetings and correspondence with members of parliament friendly and hostile, and with other groups.

For anxiety was not limited to Lancashire, nor to the employers alone, but was shared by the workers in the trade. Up in Scotland "a public Meeting of the Working Weavers, held on August 28th, resolved to draw up a MEMORIAL to be sent by express to the British Parliament". They expressed alarm "that the infant manufacture of MUSLINS should be loaded with a duty", and "resolved to open a correspondence with the Working-people of their Profession" and publish their sentiments "in the Glasgow, Edinburgh and Manchester newspapers . . .".[1]

Their alarm proved justified; paralysis began to creep over the cotton industry, and by November, Richard Townley was

[1] *Manchester Mercury*, 30th August.

writing to the *Mercury* drawing attention to "the present intire cessation from Business among the Dyers, Bleachers, and their Servants and Labourers", and suggesting that they present a petition begging the King "to end that state which throws out of employ so many thousand of industrious Manufacturers, and occasions such uncommon distress to numberless poor Families . . .".

A petition was accordingly drawn up, and more than 50,000 people signed it. The local Press reported the presentation of the petition "for the Gentlemen, Clergy, Landholders and Manufacturers (including the working-people of the Trade) signed by such a Number of People as made the Parchment as much as one Man could carry; stating that they were out of employment and at the Eve of starving, on account of the Duty last year imposed on Cottons, Linens and other goods . . . and that they must inevitably starve or quit the Kingdom unless the said Act was repealed . . .".

Fox spoke in support of the petition, and was backed by his party; Burke made an eloquent speech, calling upon "the charity and beneficence and justice of the House" and "bidding the Gentlemen to recollect that whilst they fared sumptuously every day and knew no want, these poor wretched industriously-inclined Men had not the where-with-all to supply the natural calls of the Day".

The question of the Fustian Tax had been linked by Walker and his fellow manufacturers with Pitt's unpopular Irish policy, and the petition demanded the revocation of the "reciprocal trade" act of 1784, which offered "unbounded profusion" of advantages to manufacturers in Ireland, and threatened Lancashire with the emigration of its better-off mill-owners, and disaster to their work-people.

Anti-Irish feeling was strong and widespread, and exacerbated the opposition to the government. It was a clever move to bring the question of Ireland into the campaign, for it ensured Lancashire of the support of the industrialists of the Yorkshire woollen trade, and of the rising engineering trade in the Midlands, who shared their fears of a flood of cheap goods from Ireland and would on this issue join forces in a campaign against Pitt.

Thomas Walker shared the general view; for all his independence of spirit and his broadminded international outlook, he
was a fervent protectionist. One would like to think that he had
the interests of the unfortunate Irish at heart, as well as those
of the Lancashire merchants; but it must be admitted that he
feared a setback of the cotton trade more than anything else,
and saw only this side of the question. Even when many of his
fellow industrialists welcomed Pitt's treaty of 1783 encouraging
trade with France, Walker opposed it. Free trade in a world of
brotherly love would, he conceded, be a blessing; in the immediate present and future he would look on it as a curse and
possible ruin for the people of Lancashire, who commanded his
first loyalty.

It was in this protectionist spirit that he helped to found the
General Chamber of Manufacturers in 1785. This was mainly
the result of the anti-Irish campaign, which brought together
so many industrialists of different trades, though the idea of
such an organisation had been in the minds of many of them
for some time. Josiah Wedgwood had formulated a plan for
such a body as early as 1774, and had even got his artist John
Flaxman to design a "manufacturers' Coat of Arms". Matthew
Boulton and James Watt were also keenly interested in the
organisation—which appeared to offer, among other advantages, some way of safeguarding them from the thefts of their
inventions—and later on Matthew Boulton often presided
over the meetings.[1]

A committee was set up on 3rd March, 1785—the majority
of its members cotton men, but with Wedgwood in the chair—
and the Chamber came into being; it was the first of its kind,
and the forerunner of the business associations of to-day,
though of course its functions differed in many ways—there
were, for instance, no stable working-class organisations either
great or small with which to discuss labour problems; the
manufacturing class was the one which, at this period, was
having to establish its position, and it was with a feudal
aristocracy rather than a labour movement that it had to
contend.

In the meantime, agitation for the repeal of the Fustian Tax

[1] Witt Bowden, op. cit., p. 177.

went on. Dyers and bleachers, faced with ruin, voted in the Manchester committee in favour of shutting down their plants, but the majority of the members wanted constitutional methods for redress. In January 1785 a deputation with Thomas Walker at its head was sent to confer in London with the committee of the recently appointed Board of Trade; but they got no promise of relief.

They were treated with a humiliating condescension. The government seemed to be blind to the rising power of the manufacturers, and determined to embitter them by its inconsiderate treatment of their delegates.

The *Manchester Mercury* of 19th January, gives a vivid description of Walker's experience of governmental disdain:

"Mr. Walker was at the Bar near Three Hours," it reports; "and during that long investigation supported his Testimony with a firmness and an adherence to Truth which could not be construed into Prevarication or Contradiction. The number of Cross-questions which the Chancellor put to Mr. Walker were just 174. . . . Mr. Walker, replying to a question about the Poor on the Parrish Books, remarked that there were none before the imposition of the Fustian Tax . . . and that since the Duty was imposed the home business done by his House was not in the Proportion of one to a thousand to what it used to be."

At this point, the reporter tells us, "the Noble Lord quitted his exalted Seat on the Woolsack and took refuge on the Barons' Bench, where, soon after, in Company with a Noble Duke, he comforted himself with a sound Nap. . . . The somniferious God spread his leaden Wings around their Noble Heads, and the Experiences of the 120,000 Manufacturers of Manchester sunk into a mere Vision, and became but as a Transitory Dream on an insignificant Subject."

Walker seems to have come out of the ordeal with considerable credit; the *Mercury* "regretted that the Impossibility of taking upon Memory of question and answer does not permit us to do that justice to Mr. Walker which the clearness of his Testimony, the masterly Manner of his Replies, and the excellent Language he used, most amply deserved . . .". Another witness said that Walker's evidence had been very fair and "not at all influenced by this Tax". Walker himself later described his ordeal, which seems to have been gruelling indeed.

On his return home, "a most numerous and respectable Meeting at the Exchange Coffee House agreed in voting him thanks for endeavouring to bring conviction to the minds of his Majesty's Ministers of the impolicy and ruinous tendency of this tax".

The lack of satisfaction obtained, and the cavalier treatment of their delegates, only incensed the industrial areas more.

Nation-wide activity on the part of the Chamber of Manufacturers produced a flood of more than sixty petitions to the House of Commons, denouncing both the Irish Resolutions and the excises, and at last Pitt was forced to yield on the more obnoxious features of the tax. But the Chamber did not consider this was enough, and advised its members to send more petitions.

Parliament received another deluge, and this time Pitt was forced to beat a retreat and allow a new debate on the whole question.

This took place on 12th May, 1785, and Fox led the attack.

He condemned the government representative's attitude to the delegates: "When hundreds of thousands come to our bar deprecating the continuance of a system which from their own knowledge they pronounce to be ruinous to the Manufacturers of England, he treats them with something that merits a severer term than disdain. Mr. Wedgwood . . . and Mr. Walker . . . who from opulence and every other consideration are worthy to be ranked with the best men in this house, have received from the Right Honourable Gentleman every species of ill treatment and indignity that the lowest and most degraded characters could receive, or the most contemptuous and violent could bestow on them. Can the Committee think that they know more of the Manchester Manufacturers than Mr. Richardson and Mr. Walker?"

Referring to the public feeling against the tax, Fox said that "so general a union never took place as on this occasion. So large a number of petitions never was presented from the Manufacturers on any former occasion. The voice of the whole country is there against the Resolutions." He reminded the House that Pitt had said of the India Bill, when similar petitions were presented: "Will you persist in this Bill against the voice of the people? Will you not hearken to the petitions on your table?"—"It was ever my opinion, sir," said Fox, "that Petitions should be heard and most sincerely attended to (though not that they should always be implicitly complied with)."

On the eve of this debate, Manchester had sent a deputation consisting, again, of Thomas Walker and John Richardson, to London to bring some last-minute pressure to bear, should it be needed. Whether or not their lobbying just tipped the scales is not known, but at all events, when Pitt admitted defeat and announced the repeal of the hated tax, the delegates' home town took for granted that their presence had helped to win the victory. Subscriptions were immediately raised for a presentation, and a grand procession of welcome was arranged by the local authorities; we learn in the *Mercury* of 17th May that "the Procession for the Meeting the Delegates of the Fustian Trade on their return from London being fixed for this day, it is requested that those Gentlemen who means (*sic*) to attend on Horseback, will assemble in St. Anne's Square, precisely at 8 o'clock in the Morning, dressed agreeable to their own Inclinations". Gentlemen who "purpose dining with the Delegates and Committee are desired to sign their names".

A further notice announced the route of the Procession, adding that "it is hoped that the Inhabitants of the aforementioned Streets will cause them to be watered in the Morning of that Day if no Rain should fall in the meantime". The words were given of "a Catch to be sung at this Day's Festival".

The *Manchester Chronicle* of 21st May carried a long report of the procession, which must indeed have been a splendid sight—though, sad to relate, "the weather was not favourable".

But rain or no rain, the general enthusiasm was not damped, as, according to the reporter, "early in the morning the town began to be alive", and "by eight o'clock the procession to receive the delegates was in motion and proceeded to meet them", going along the road towards London in the following order:

First, "six Firemen, with blue and buff cockades"—these were George Washington's colours, and very much in vogue

with the Whigs on all state occasions. "Six Javelin Men. A
Trumpeter. Fustian Cutters with flags and various mottoes.
Packers with emblems of their trade. Fustian shearers, Dressers
and Calenderers, with flags. Dyers with flags and various
mottoes. A band. Dragoons on horseback. Master Fustian
shearers, with sashes made of Jean. Master Velvet dressers and
Calenderers with buff and blue sashes. Whitsters, Pattern Card
makers, and Dyers dressed in Devonshire brown velveret coats,
buff waistcoats, black breeches, mazarin blue sashes with roses
of pink. Olive flag of Fustian plain, motto *Truth*."

Then followed a mixed consignment of "witnesses, foreign
clerks (carrying the motto RESPECT) javelin men and trumpeters"; then representatives of the Chamber of Manufacturers
with their flag, then warehouse men, then "martial musick"
with a buff and blue flag, motto FRIENDS OF MANCHESTER; then,
two by two, gentlemen of the town and neighbourhood, followed by more javelin men, the town's band of music, beadles,
the Deputy Constable, and other constables in a chariot; next,
the Lord of the Manor (the Sir Oswald Moseley of the day) in a
chariot alone, followed by the secretary of the Fustian Tax
Committee, the "bearer of the Repeal", who carried a banner
inscribed "Eighty Thousand" (being the number of petitioners
for the repeal), more marshals, stewards, treasurers, javelin
men, trumpeters; finally, preceded by a flag announcing
"Freedom Restored", the two delegates made their appearance,
each in a phaeton, wearing "uniforms of Scarlett, with Sashes
of rich pink and white Silk".

The delegates, of course, only made the return journey, after
being met by the procession four miles along the London road.

At the point where they were waiting, the Constables of the
town delivered an address of thanks to them, and then the
procession turned round and "returned in the most excellent
order", arriving in the town again at midday.

The *Chronicle* says that "they then proceeded through all the
principal streets, where every window was filled with spectators
anxious to view the tribute paid to gentlemen, who, by their
abilities, industry and perseverance, have emancipated the
town from shackles which must for ever have cramped its
trade". When the procession reached Salford, there was a

C

presentation of silver plate and of a handsome silver cup from Bolton ("the original seat of the fustian industry" as the inscription remarked). The leading Churchman of the town, the Reverend Mr. Kenyon, made a long speech, in the course of which he congratulated the worthy delegates and the gentlemen of the Committee "on the happy Repeal of the odious and oppressive tax on Fustians, and thanked them for their eminent services for the good of the country".

The reporter commented that "the management, regularity and elegant appearance of the whole procession at once surprised and delighted the Spectators, and did great honour to the Managers, by far exceeding any expectations formed on the occasion".

At four o'clock they all went to "an elegant dinner, and the day was spent with the most social harmony by all ranks of people".

Walker's family rejoiced greatly, and later in the day showed their feelings by shooting off a round from a toy cannon belonging to Thomas junior, the elder son. Its faint reverberation mingled with the cheers of the crowds and the strains of the Catch for "the Day's Festival"—"This Day we all will spend with glee, for Fustians are from Taxes free, and Merry, merry we will be . . .".

And so dusk fell on a happy day for Manchester; and for Thomas Walker, on what was probably the happiest day in his whole life.

## CHAPTER IV

# CHURCH AND KING AGAINST DISSENTERS
## (1786-1790)

THE years following the Fustian Tax battle were on the whole peaceful and uneventful. The English public had little idea that a social upheaval of incalculable importance was preparing just across the Channel, and during the period just before the French Revolution the only causes to stir national excitement were the illness of George III and the trial of Warren Hastings.

Young William Pitt had the reins of office firmly in his hands, supported by a few Whigs, the bulk of the Tories, and the whole of the Court except for the Prince of Wales and his close friends. Fox led the opposition, with Burke, Wyndham, and Dundas as his chief right-hand men, and Sheridan and Grey on his left. The important issues which were later to split the Whigs into a party divided against itself had not yet arisen, and parliamentary debates were calm and comparatively humdrum.

In the north of England times were busy and relatively prosperous, at any rate for the manufacturers. Walker's business was going smoothly, and he was doing well both at home and in the foreign market, as he had established good connections with some of the biggest firms on the Continent, particularly in Germany and Italy. His home life was happy, and he had a wide circle of friends which included not only the local Radicals —Dr. Ferriar, Thomas Cooper, Samuel Jackson and other distinguished Mancunians—but many important politicians and intellectuals. During the struggle against Pitt's taxes he got to know Lord Derby very well, and through him met Fox and other Whig leaders. Derby became godfather to one of the Walker children, invited Thomas to stay at Knowsley, took him to plays at Richmond House and introduced him to the Whig Club in 1788. He wrote him spicy letters reporting the latest gossip about the King's illness and the Regency question.

"The Prince behaves perfectly well, and sticks steadily to his friends," he reported, referring to the Prince of Wales' connection with Fox's group; "so that your *friend* Pitt will, I hope, very soon be reduced to a private and subordinate situation." And much more in the same vein.

That Walker's friends greatly respected and esteemed him is very evident from the many letters he had from Lord Derby, from Fox, from Lord Grey, Josiah Wedgwood, Dr. Priestley, Frend and other divines, politicians and poets. They often asked him for advice and information and help; even more often they thanked him for what he had already done for them.[1]

His time was mainly taken up with his business, his family, and a limited amount of political activity; it was difficult at this time to get much public interest in the cause nearest to his heart—the cause of parliamentary reform. In this short period of comparative calm there were no burning questions, no battles to be rushed into. The American war was over; and though the people might be stirring—pondering over the British defeats, and the price they had paid in money and in blood for King George's vain attempts to prevent the American people winning their independence—though many were asking themselves whether in fact a change of régime was not overdue in England too, industrial and social unrest did not ruffle the surface of English life.

When a new storm blew up, in 1789, it was not over the question of reform, or revolution, or Ireland, but over a matter which we to-day can hardly conceive to be a cause of such bitterness and bad blood. It was over the request for a repeal of the Test and Corporation Acts, which had for a hundred and twenty years past imposed grave and most unjust restrictions on the Dissenters of the country, and which the Established Church seemed to consider as absolutely necessary to its own safety, and well-being.

During the previous decade there had been comparatively little open hostility by the "high" Churchmen (so called to distinguish them from the Evangelicals) to nonconformists, owing to the fact that the latter had not tried to assert their rights, and had kept silent on controversial issues. We know

[1] Jerrold, op. cit., pp. 16-18.

that Jacobites and Hanoverians met and tippled together at Shaw's Punch House, Churchmen and Dissenters alike; while there was no hope of reform there was no reason for anger. Political and religious friction arose only, and rarely, when provoked by commercial or administrative competition.[1]

After several years of relative peace, nonconformists up and down the country thought it might be a good moment to bring up the question of a repeal of the oppressive out-dated Acts.

As Fox argued, on 8th May, 1789, they had originally "been introduced with a view to exclude Papists *only* from office. The Dissenters had cordially . . . consented to their own exclusion thinking *that* a lesser evil than to leave the door open to papists." (Was it, one wonders, really necessary for Fox to justify the Acts at any time, or on any pretext?—they would have been a blot on the record of any government at whatever period.) The Whig leader indignantly asked the House: "Would you take advantage of their patriotism . . . and make a perpetual exclusion against themselves? . . . Was it thus the Church would reward the services they had done her, in the day of her distress?"

Resolutions passed at countless meetings of Dissenters at this time were reasonable enough, declaring as often as not that they "entertained no principles which are inconsistent with the welfare of the present Government". But that they felt their humiliation sharply, is shown by the declaration of a nonconformist group at Devizes in Wiltshire: "We conceive it a manifest injustice to be incapacitated from holding offices of trust, honour and emolument," they say, "especially as no religious tests are required for holding the offices of Scotland or Ireland." And they protest at the fact that those in office who do not take the Sacrament according to the rites of the Church of England, are punished "by a very heavy penalty and such severe disabilities as ought to be annexed to the most atrocious crimes". Adding that "the first George honestly struggled to remove the opprobrious distinction which debased the Dissenters"—in contrast to the glaringly partisan attitude of George III.

[1] Jerrold, op. cit., pp. 17-18.

In Manchester, one voice was raised in a letter to the *Chronicle* calling fellow-citizens "to join the numerous and respectable society of dissenters in and about London, by entering similar resolutions [for a repeal]". . . . "This is no party business, thank God. Men of all political descriptions have seen its propriety and joined in its support," said the writer, and proposed that a public meeting be held, to help on the cause.

We do not know if this was organised, but if it was we may be sure that Thomas Walker was co-operating, as he was wholeheartedly behind the movement for the repeal of the Acts. This did not improve his relations with the local reactionaries and the established clergy, of whom he had a poor opinion which he took no trouble to disguise, and of whom he wrote: "their salaries and sinecures depend upon the continuance of the public error" and "they take care that the people shall not be undeceived; and brand with 'heresy and innovation' all those who express their doubts of a position, which, however vehemently asserted, has never yet been proved".

Up to this period, Walker says, "the bickerings between the Friends to Liberty and the idolaters of authority in Manchester were carried on with a spirit of opposition indeed, but not of hatred . . .".

However the clergy looked on "liberality toward the Dissenters" as an act of open hostility against themselves.

"Sermons were everywhere preached, against all who favoured the repeal of these acts of Parliament"; and this Walker considered "as pernicious a practice as any that fanaticism or arbitrary power have ever employed: for the doctrines delivered to an ignorant multitude from the pulpit are not to be repelled by opposite doctrines, like fair public or printed arguments, but are like wounds in the dark which become fatal before a remedy can be procured".

It was the Dissenters' campaign in 1789, in Walker's view, that marked "the commencement of party violence". On a former occasion their application to Parliament had only been rejected by twenty votes, and their chances of success now seemed considerable. This seriously alarmed the clergy.

According to Walker, "the fears of those who cried out 'the Church in danger' became as wild and absurd as ever they were in the days of Sacheverell and his party".[1]

Anti-dissenter leaflets were printed, in which no pains were spared to blacken those who were trying to obtain a repeal of the Acts. One, so scurrilous as possibly to defeat its own ends, ran as follows:

"And it came to pass in the thirtieth Year of the Reign of George the Third, who was anointed King of Great Britain that the Set of People called Dissenters (who prospered in the Land) conspired together, 'Let us chuse out among ourselves a King, Governments, Rulers, and Men of cunning Devices, and let us depose, dethrone and put to death this King. . . . And moreover we will deny Christ and confess Arius, Socinius and Pelagius and we will entirely overthrow the Brittanic Constitution.' These things they will so do, and many more, to make their names famous throughout the Earth."[2]

As well as distributing leaflets, the "High Church party" decided to advance its cause by holding a meeting. The church-wardens of about half a dozen churches approached Edward Place the Boroughreeve ("a circumstance sufficiently evincing the activity of the clergy upon this occasion" commented Walker) and asked him to call a public meeting, "to consider of and consult about, the impropriety of the application . . . to obtain a repeal of those salutary laws, the great bulwarks and barriers for a century and upwards of our glorious Constitution in Church and State . . .".[3]

The Meeting was advertised by a handbill urging all loyal churchgoers to "remember who trampled upon and made shipwreck of both Church and State in the last Century, and guard against the Repetition of the like Dreadful Scene", and to "attend the Meeting tomorrow (2nd February) between 10 and 11 o'clock and give your decided Disapprobation of the Measures pursuing by the Dissenters".

Thomas Walker, convinced that the freedom of Dissenters was bound up with the freedom of all citizens, went along with

---

[1] Walker, *Review of some Political Events in Manchester* (1794), p. 11.

[2] Manchester Reference Library pamphlets, 1789.

[3] Manchester Reference Library pamphlets, 2nd February, 1790.

Thomas Cooper, George Lloyd (a barrister friend), and one or two other democrats, to the function. It had been announced as a public meeting, but "the room was nearly filled by the adherents of the High Church Party before any others could be admitted".

"To increase the solemnity," Walker wrote, "the Clergy attended in their gowns and cassocks. Some opposition was made to the manner in which the meeting had been called, and the indecent stratagem by which the room had been previously filled; and it was particularly objected that, according to the rule of 1788, the Boroughreeve had not the right to call any meeting of the inhabitants except a general one."

Thomas and his friends sat down to listen, but were soon exasperated by the proceedings: "The clamour of the High Church men was violent beyond description. Resolutions prepared beforehand were put into the hands of the Boroughreeve while he was in the midst of his speech . . . and these resolutions, seconded even before they were read, were as hastily passed, in the noise and confusion which prevailed. Till the next morning when they were printed, it is probable that few of the persons present understood a syllable of what had been voted."

The resolutions were published under the heading "CONSTITUTION AGAINST INNOVATION" and with the comment that "the *real* friends of this Town and Neighbourhood, Members of the ESTABLISHED CHURCH and firm in the OLD CAUSE, have again an opportunity of congratulating their Fellow Citizens (this Day) on the complete overthrow of the PROTESTANT DISSENTERS. . . . And notwithstanding the Legions of Dissenting Congregations, headed by their respective Pastors (who so indecently *foisted* themselves, *uninvited*, upon the Meeting) they were ROUTED and DISAPPOINTED."

There were eight resolutions, seven of them saying almost exactly the same thing, in slightly different words: "That the Acts give Strength and Permanence to our excellent Constitution, and ought to be transmitted unimpaired to the latest Posterity."

The whole business infuriated the Radicals who were at the meeting. "A conduct like this", wrote Walker, "gave extreme disgust to myself and others, who without being partial to any body of men, wished to see those of every religious persuasion placed on an equal footing.

"Religious differences would soon become of little importance, if all men were left to go to Heaven their own way, without persecution or proscription for their opinions. These sentiments prevailed among a great number of the inhabitants, who adjourned the same day (3rd February) to a different house [Shaw's Punch House] and protested against these High-Church proceedings."[1]

For some time after the turbulent meeting its echoes were heard in the Town; each of the conflicting sides issued broadsheets which were sold in the streets. The democrats' was entitled *A Priest's Confession* and went to the tune of *The Vicar of Bray*:

> When Test and Corporation Acts are subject of dispute, Sir,
> I dare not argue to the point, but theirs I will refute, Sir,
> And this is Church I will maintain until my dying day, Sir,
> Whatever arguments are used, *my* argument's Huzza, Sir.
>
> I'll go to simple Neddy Place, and pat his cheek and wheedle,
> I'll get him for to say the grace while I do play the fiddle;
> And this is Church, etc. . . .
>
> If at the Meeting he can't read, we sure can make him mutter,
> We'll put a paper in his hand and raise a mighty sputter,
> And this is Church, etc. . . .
>
> With Lord St. David's at our head we'll hoot all Reformation,
> And such as will not join with us we'll send 'em to Damnation.
> And this is Church, etc. . . .

The "Church and King" men retorted with a *Dissenter's Ditty* about the exodus of the democrats from the meeting, with special references to their "generals":

> Unequal matched, by Churchmen scratched,
> We fled the first Huzza, Sirs,
> Obliged to yield, we left the field
> To *Priestcraft* and its cause, Sirs.

[1] Walker, *Review*, pp. 11-14.

*Chorus*
With crests erect and fierce Aspect,
We met our Foes in fight, Sirs,
But all our Might, joined to our LIGHT
Could not command success, Sirs.

The second verse contains a reference to George Lloyd ("alias
Noso Conicus, lately a member of the Church of England but
now a disciple of the AP Cooper who has made him a Dissenter
and convinced him he has no soul"). Then comes an allusion to
Walker ("a follower of P—stl—y"):

Next Tommy Tax, that Lad of Wax,
If Charly F—x said Yea, Sirs,
Would souse the Church and Calvin lurch,
    And after that, Huzza, Sirs.

Verse III seems to suggest that Cooper was the moving
spirit among the Radicals (he was, indeed, one of the liveliest
minds of the time, in Manchester or anywhere else):

Apostle Coop did head a Troop
    Of valiant Men, 'tis true, Sirs,
But Cooper foiled, his rout recoiled,
And fled to Billy Shaw's, Sirs.

Those responsible for the meeting must have felt it needed
some justification, for they published a wordy leaflet about it,
soon after, in the form of a "Dialogue between a Respectable
Farmer not versed in the merits of an Hotel Contention and a
Town's Gentleman of Minuter Information".

The Farmer began by asking "what caused so much turbul-
ence at the Meeting?" and the Gentleman replied, "The
Presbyterians' obtrusion. They were industriously collected in
vast numbers ... they most impudently attended, with the fullest
confidence in carrying everything their own way."

The Farmer wanted to know "what occasioned so much
precipitation in passing the resolutions, and an inattention to
two or three gentlemen who first earnestly requested a hearing";
he was told that "a deep laid scheme had come to the ears of the
President ... the end of which would have been outrage and
riot ...".

Hence "the Boroughreeve's very urgent motive for coming to the question at once".

To the Farmer's query whether "the Gentlemen intended as Orators were persons of consequence", the Gentleman said, yes they were, and gave a thumbnail sketch of some of them:

"That little man [Cooper] with a singular aspect has sterling abilities. He was brought up to the law . . . but his principal business at present is that of a whitster. He has an unhappy propensity to engage in all party disputes. . . . He often moves an investigation into the expenditure of the Town's money. His interpositions are generally impertinent, disapproved and dangerous."

George Lloyd was described as "that tall ruddy man with a bald head . . . by profession a lawyer, not of very intense application. He has lately contracted an itching for oratory. No man suffered more than himself when he went away with his undisgorged speech."

But, of all the unflattering portraits, that of Thomas Walker is the most defamatory, and reveals the spiteful feeling against him among his opponents: "That lusty tall black-visaged man is a merchant, long practised in elocution and in laboriously feeding party flames. He is arrogant, ambitious, choleric, and full of asperity. He is an excellent dab at perverting meanings, particularly when expressed by the word Innovation."[1]

In spite of all the efforts of the dissenters' champions the Bill for the Repeal of the Test Acts was rejected when brought before Parliament at the beginning of March 1790. The defeat was a great disappointment to the liberal-minded, but a cause of delight to reactionaries all over the country—including King George, who wrote to Pitt on 3rd March, expressing his joy at the rejection.[2]

To mark the occasion the Manchester Tories and clergy formed their local "Church and King Club"—later nicknamed the "Tythe and Tax Club". Walker tells us that its first meeting "was held on the 13th of March 1790, with solemnities as ridiculous as any to be found in the history of Toryism. They wore uniforms with the representation of the Old Church at

[1] Manchester Reference Library pamphlets, 1790.
[2] Holland Rose, *Pitt and George III*, p. 221.

Manchester engraved on their buttons. They appointed a Committee for the admission of members of suitable lives and conversations, and struck medals to commemorate the fact that the repeal had been negatived. Everything said in favour of liberty or liberality was to these gentlemen a declaration of War against the Constitution in Church and State. The standing toast of their club, and in their private societies was 'Church and King, and down with the Rump'."

Walker and his friends felt the need to organise some society "to oppose the intolerant and slavish doctrines which were daily instilled into the people". Accordingly, in October, 1790, a number of public-spirited and liberal-minded manufacturers and professional men agreed to form the Manchester Constitutional Society. Their aims were published in a declaration which stated among other things, that "the authority of the Government can only be derived from the consent of those governed; and that the happiness of the latter ought to be the sole end and aim of government; that Actions only, and not Opinions, are the proper objects of civil jurisdiction; that the People of Great Britain are not fairly represented in Parliament, and that the representation requires a speedy and effectual reform".[1]

Though the society had sprung from the defence of the rights of the Dissenters, it will be seen that it proposed to campaign for the defence of all civil rights. Its objectives and its methods might appear very innocent to the average reader; the need for reform had indeed been proclaimed by many respectable bodies and individuals—including Pitt himself—in very similar terms, not many years before.

But something very important had happened in the meantime, which gave the word Reform a new significance. The taking of the Bastille on 14th July, 1789, and the change of government in France with its new and revolutionary measures and its proclamation of the Rights of Man, these things had jolted England and stirred a new interest in social questions. The majority of the British took a not unsympathetic but detached view of events in France, while many welcomed the downfall of the absolute monarchy and the installation of a

[1] Walker, *Review*, p. 29.

more democratic régime. Walker was typical of his countrymen when he expressed pleasure that the French nation "has displayed to the world the glorious example of renouncing all schemes of ambition and conquest and avowing a system of UNIVERSAL BENEVOLENCE", just as Fox spoke for the progressive Whigs when he exclaimed "How much the greatest thing it is that ever happened in the world, and how much the best!"[1]

While not aware of the full implications of the revolution, the British people realised that something had happened which was important to them as well as to the French; France was putting her house in order, and they could too—in their own way, of course. With the new stimulus, interest in reform, which had lapsed for so long, began to revive.

Manchester was only one among many towns where societies were formed to promote the cause. The aims of the Constitutional Society were very much the same as those of the Popular Societies at Norwich, Sheffield, Derby and other places. Like them, the Manchester group met regularly, in one of the many public houses, to have discussions, read papers, publish and distribute pamphlets, and to organise an occasional dinner. The members were mostly middle class and professional men, although the society was open to all, regardless of politics or creed. In its early days the members would have found it hard to believe that within a year they would have become branded as dangerous and subversive conspirators. In 1789 life was comparatively calm, and the deep-rooted hostility of the Church and King Club and its friends in authority was, though very strong, not yet directed to wrecking and ruining the Radicals.

[1] *Memorials of Fox*, ed. Russell, ii, p. 361.

## CHAPTER V

# LIBEL (1790)

IN spite of religious and political dissension, Thomas Walker's popularity was still great enough, five years after the Fustian Tax battles, for him to be appointed Borough-reeve of Manchester. This office, though it did not entail very much activity or responsibility, carried with it a great deal of prestige. As mentioned already, the Boroughreeve was the chief police officer, answerable for the law and order of the town; in fact the constables under him did the work and his main function was to superintend them, to call (or refuse to call) public meetings, and in general to represent and preside over the community.

The important thing was for him, and the jury supporting him, to be popular and reliable people. As one of the Stewards of the Manor, in his *Charge to the Jury* in 1788, remarked: "It is of no publick consideration whatever what religious persuasion the Boroughreeve, the Constables or other Officers hold—all we want, and all that are necessary, are sensible, respectable, steady, upright, active Officers."

Self-evident as this may seem, the statement is impressive coming as it did from an American emigré barrister, William Roberts, who had settled in Manchester not long before. He himself had strong party feelings, which he suppressed at that time, though unfortunately they appeared before long only too clearly.

It is a sign of the times that he should have expressed himself thus in 1788; and that in an edition of his speech published in 1793, the wording was changed to read: "Members of the Jury must be men who testify an affectionate loyalty to the King, a veneration for the Constitution, and a proper sense of the blessings which flow from them; without which no man ought to be invested with any public trust whatever."

However, in 1790, when Walker was appointed Borough-reeve, a healthy mixture of political opinions, including a

strong tinge of Radicalism, was represented on the jury. The
list of the Court Leet that year contains the names of Matthew
Falkner, the progressive printer and bookseller, as "Market-
Looker for the Assize of Bread", and his partner Samuel Birch
as "Scavenger for Shudehill and the Top of Market Street
Lane". Walker's brother Richard was foreman of the jury in
1791; William Paul, later a member of the Constitutional
Society, was a foreman at Easter, 1789.

One of the less congenial characters in public office was the
violent die-hard Richard Unite—"Officer to distribute Rent
Charge from Collyhurst, and Deputy Constable".[1] He made his
way by blustering, bullying and embezzling, in and out of
different civic positions; he was later appointed salaried Overseer of the Poor, but was in the end exposed as the scoundrel he
was, and dismissed. During the years following Walker's
Boroughreeveship he appeared many times, like a persistent
gadfly, following and stinging Thomas more or less harmfully
whenever he could, through sheer hatred of progressive or
liberal ideas.

The magistrates of the town and the justices of the peace had
no say in the councils of the Court Leet. But one gathers that
they were influential behind the scenes. The Reverend Dr.
Maurice Griffith and his son, the Reverend John, both justices
of the peace, were two arch-intriguers, always busy plotting the
downfall of Dissenters or democrats, such as Walker and his
friends, whom they could not bear. But in the main, at Easter
and throughout most of 1790, none of this animosity was
apparent. Only once, at the end of that year, was a note of discord publicly sounded in Manchester—faint, but like a disagreeable warning of worse things to come.

The fact that Walker, a well-known radical, had been officially
approved by the vast majority of his fellow-citizens to be their
chief representative, rankled deeply with some of the local
Tories.

The trouble was, of course, that it was not easy to pick a hole
in his character. He was a good husband and father, a kind
employer, an efficient and trustworthy man of business, prominent on all sorts of boards and committees where he carried out

[1] Manchester Court Leet Records (1788-90).

his duties as chairman or member regularly and conscientiously.

One of his many interests was the local hospital, which had been founded in 1752, and which by 1790 consisted of the Infirmary, Lunatic Hospital and Asylum. The board, on which Thomas sat, was very active and held lengthy meetings four times a year.

Developments of the medical services were under discussion in June, 1790, when it was decided to build an isolation ward "to be set apart and kept ready in case any in-patient should be seized with a fever or other infectious disorder during his stay at the Infirmary".[1]

At the same time it was decided to double the medical and surgical stuff, and arrange for each of the six physicians and six surgeons to undertake alike the care of in-patients, out-patients and lunatics. A man and a woman were also appointed to superintend the men's and women's wards respectively.

There was a certain amount of Tory opposition to these measures, which involved considerable spending, but which the Whigs on the committee thought worthwhile, and indeed essential.

The "high church party" agitated ceaselessly for cuts in expenditure on the hospital, and the matter of raising and spending money was well aired over a considerable period in the *Manchester Herald*, a year or two later. We are told by this newspaper, for instance, in its weekly paragraph "News of the Infirmary" of "Charity Sermons preached for the benefit of our Infirmary . . . by the Rector of St. Mary's Church" and a great many more by ministers in dissenting chapels. An editorial note observes "with inexpressible pleasure . . . the astounding collections making at the churches and chapels in this town and more than twenty miles round . . . in support of that most useful and extensive charity . . . and the late alterations and improvements—necessary and important as any that have happened for some time to this very populous country".[2]

Although a few rectors preached sermons to raise money for the improvements, a number of clergymen disapproved of and publicly denounced the progressive administration for its spending. The Secretary of the Hospital Board, James Hilton,

[1] Brockbank, op. cit., p. 32.    [2] *Manchester Herald*, 21st March, 1792.

an attorney, answered their charge by an invitation to these clergy to attend the next board meeting, and lodge an official complaint. This invitation was declined: "Though we are still far from approving the expensive measures adopted," they said, "we would rather . . . bear the reluctance of our own private judgments than disturb the public peace and harmony of the board by fruitless expostulations. . . ."

This was answered by the Infirmary Committee with a full report on the expenditure and the reasons for it, drawn up by the physicians and surgeons (including Mr. Killer, the House Surgeon). They remarked that it was "a false economy to withhold drugs", and claimed that the spending was fully justified and indeed necessary.

\* \* \*

It was an argument about economy and expense on the Hospital Board that led to an episode which gave Thomas Walker some annoyance and revealed the depth of the latent prejudice against him in some quarters, in spite of his high standing in the town. William Roberts, the one time Court Leet Steward, was one of those who shared the views of the clergy and disliked what he considered unnecessary extravagance on behalf of the lower classes. He also heartily disliked Walker. The two factors, added to the reason that Walker usually got his way, while he, Roberts, was ignored, induced in him a state of mind in which nothing he could say or do against the Boroughreeve seemed to him bad enough.

At Michaelmas, 1790, the Hospital Board met as usual, and a discussion took place (to quote a contemporary report) "on the appointment of an additional number of Medical Assistants to attend upon that Institution: a measure which was thought by many to be very necessary, and fit to be adopted, on account of the increased number of patients, and the larger demand for Medical Assistance which that increase had occasioned".

"Many Gentlemen assembled upon that occasion," we are told, "and delivered their sentiments upon the subject then under discussion, with the freedom which became them. It happened that Mr. Walker was of the opinion that more Medical Assistance was, under the then circumstances . . .

D

necessary, in order to promote further the ends of that Institution. Mr. Roberts was of a different opinion. Each of them endeavoured to sustain his opinion by argument, but it does not appear that anything passed . . . that could impress even the sorest-minded man in the world with an idea that any affront, insult or injury was intended to be offered by Mr. Walker to Mr. Roberts. . . ."

It appears that Roberts thought otherwise; it also seems that he made a very poor speech on that occasion, for, meeting James Hilton later in a coffee-house, he complained that his friends at dinner had been rallying him about it. "The company had paid him a very poor compliment to think that he could not speak as well as Walker," he said. When Hilton tried to soothe him, he refused to be appeased, called Walker a number of unflattering names, and said he was "a proud, haughty, overbearing, imperious fellow, and that the first opportunity he had he would quarrel with him. . . . The town gave Walker credit for being a very clever fellow . . . but he was a passionate haughty man." He talked about challenging him, said that Walker had contradicted him at the Infirmary, and he "was very sorry he did not call him a damned liar. . . ". Hilton was roused by this to defend Walker as, in his opinion, "a man of great consequence, a very active townsman, and a very good one too".

However, Roberts was determined to have his quarrel, and he found an opportunity—or rather, made it—at the annual "Revolution Dinner" of 5th November, 1790.

This dinner was one of the few social events in which Whigs and Tories, Dissenters and churchmen could now meet and mix comparatively amicably. It was held every year to celebrate the so-called revolution of 1688—when William of Orange arrived in England and introduced the new constitution, which, according to the bills advertising the dinner, "secured the civil Rights of the People, established the Protestant Religion, and seated the Brunswick Family on the Throne of Great Britain".

There had been a specially grand dinner in 1788, when invitations had been issued by Matthew Falkner the printer to "every sincere Friend to the British Constitution" to celebrate "an Occasion of which every Briton, from the Throne to the Cottage, enjoys the Benefit at this Moment". In the account of that centenary commemoration we read that a hundred and thirty of "the principal gentlemen of Manchester sat down to dinner after the ringing of bells and firing of the military in St. Anne's Square". The night before there had been "a ball and supper at the Assembly Rooms, on which occasion the ladies displayed orange coloured ribbons". Orange (William III's colour), the blue-and-buff of Washington, and the true blue of the Tories mingled more harmoniously than usual, or possibly than ever again.

In spite of the undercurrents of political friction, the Revolution Dinner of 1790 was still an occasion for a convivial evening for Manchester's leading citizens, whatever their views.

By general consent Boroughreeve Walker was in the chair, dressed in buff and blue, as were many of the company. There were sixty or seventy gentlemen, at two tables.

The atmosphere of the party is best conveyed by the verbatim report of the court case which followed it. George Lloyd is giving evidence.

Q. Did Mr. Walker conduct himself with impartiality and decorum and as a gentleman should, placed in such a situation?

A. Perfectly so; with the utmost propriety. . . . A very agreeable pleasant meeting it was, till about one hour after dinner.

As was usual at these functions, after the dinner singing was the order of the day, and "there were four hired Catch-Singers" to lead off.

"After some catches," Mr. Lloyd tells us, "the High Sheriff was desired to sing a song; he sang one called 'Liberty Hall'.

"Then Mr. Walker was desired to call upon some gentleman to sing 'The Vicar of Bray'," and "a little while after, Mr. Wood came up and desired Mr. Walker to call upon Mr. Taylor to sing the song of 'Billy Pitt the Tory', saying that he sung it very well." According to Lloyd, this was "a common popular song . . . very much in use", and in proposing it "Mr. Walker was merely the instrument for the pleasure of the company".

But "very soon after that was called for, before Mr. Taylor began to sing, Mr. Roberts got up and made some objection, stating that he thought it a party song and not proper to be sung there. . . . Mr. George Philips seconded Mr. Roberts' Motion. . . . This occasioned a good deal of noise in the room, some calling out that they would have the song; while that noise was going on, Mr. Taylor began another song, 'Rule Britannia'."

"During the singing of it," said Lloyd, "many gentlemen came up to Mr. Walker and desired he would persist in calling for the song 'Billy Pitt the Tory', for they were sure a majority would support him in it. . . ." Walker, sensing trouble, very properly declined.

Notwithstanding, Roberts, raring for his quarrel, came up to him and starting off in an abusive tone: "Mr. Borough-reeve——"

Thomas corrected him: "Sir, I am no Boroughreeve here— I am the Chairman of this meeting." Roberts immediately barked out: "Sir, in future I shall never address you by that or any other title, God damn you!" He went back to his seat, but before sitting down added: "But you shall hear from me!" To which Walker answered: "Very well."

Soon after the incident Roberts left, presumably satisfied at having caused a public stir, however small, and at annoying Walker. The company around were mystified: one diner asked another. "What can Mr. Roberts possibly have said to Mr. Walker that makes him look so damnation poisonous at him?" According to others giving evidence later, "Mr. Walker appeared to be in great anger and very much agitated", and Mr. Roberts "when he went away from Mr. Walker seemed full of anger and his face very much flushed".

After the fracas, one witness, Edward Grant, Walker's brother-in-law, said he persuaded the singer Taylor to start another song, saying "You will make yourself Enemies and no Friends—it is a Party business". And amid all the bustle he began singing "Rule Britannia", without objections from anyone, "as it always is in England", said Mr. Grant. And "in a little while the harmony of the meeting was restored and we continued together some time".

However, there was no harmony in Roberts' mind. He did not lose a moment in pursuing the quarrel he had chosen to pick.

As soon as he got home he sat down and wrote Walker an extremely abusive letter saying that he "trembles not at the fiercest blasts of your temper", and telling him that "as a Chairman you have acted with folly; as a Gentleman I have received from you impertinence unprovoked".

The correspondence that followed is worth mentioning, although its subject matter is trivial, for the light it throws on Roberts' blindly prejudiced reactionary mind, in contrast to the reasonable and calm attitude of Walker. The latter answered the outburst with a short note claiming that his conduct had been strictly proper, and that he was prepared to justify it in whatever manner Roberts pleased. This enraged Roberts, and he wrote off a second, even longer and more abusive tirade, asking "does your blazing imagination dazzle you into a belief that you are in the Chair still?", rambling on about their respective situations, hinting darkly about the "odium and guilt" of resorting to a challenge, and concluding with the words "I am ready to meet you". To all of which Walker replied with a polite but curt refusal to call upon him. This brought forth another torrent of invective to the effect that Roberts had "no objection to meet him . . . appoint a place and time . . . whenever you think proper and wherever, except at your own house".

Walker replied, with excusable impatience, in four lines, that he would give himself no more trouble about Roberts. A fourth tirade he returned unopened. Roberts sent it again, by three friends; Walker told the trio that no answer was necessary after his former reply.

Roberts, then, neither having challenged, nor failed to challenge, and feeling excessively injured at the return of his unopened letter, forced the reading matter in it on to Walker and the public by having the whole correspondence printed in the local Press. "It is a painful duty that I owe myself to be under the necessity of intruding on the public," he writes, "being obliged either to communicate this answer to Mr. Walker by publication, or submit it to be treated with contemptuous silence." Walker replied by publishing a dignified account of what, according to him, happened at the dinner and after. On seeing this Roberts returned to the attack in the

Press, "most solemnly and seriously declaring before God and the World that Walker's behaviour was overbearing, insulting and haughty to an extreme degree". He added that he had expected Walker to meet him at 8 o'clock that morning, but his message "standing unanswered will stamp a proper impression on his conduct and entitle him to an epithet or two . . . which I have not the venom to name, but which his own Consciousness must supply".

Walker retorted, for the last time, with a leaflet, eight hundred to a thousand of which were printed for him by Charles Wheeler, the more progressive of the two Manchester publishers (Falkner, the Radical, as yet did no business on this scale).

In this leaflet Walker declares that "if Mr. Roberts can *prove* anything he (Walker) has said to be erroneous *even in a single instance* Mr. Walker will meet Mr. Roberts at any time and place Mr. Roberts may think proper to appoint". But if he can not Roberts "must stand convicted of FALSEHOOD before the Public".

The immediate result of this was an almost incredible action on Roberts' part; he wrote (according to his servant Thomas Nelson "in less than a minute and a half") a most scurrilous handbill, sent it to Harrop, the Tory printer, and two hours later, as the papers came off the press, posted them up with Nelson's help all over Manchester, on doors and gateposts, "against the walls and windows of coffee houses", everywhere— and even thrust copies "under the door of Mr. Walker, for the purpose of galling him and his family with the sight of such indecent and venomous matter as it contains . . .".

The publication ran as follows:

MR. THOMAS WALKER
commenced his virulence against me like a BULLY
Has conducted it like a                 FOOL
Has acted in it like a                   SCOUNDREL
Has ended it like a                      COWARD
At last has turned                       BLACKGUARD
And unworthy of association with, or notice of any Gentleman who regards his own character.

WILLIAM ROBERTS

The author was inordinately proud of this effort. He said to someone: "Who knows but Mr. Pitt may hear of this!" He made sure, at any rate, that all Manchester heard of it; besides posting up the bills he pressed them on all and sundry he met in the streets and in friends' houses. At one card party, when it was suggested "it was not a proper place, before the Ladies, to talk about a subject of that sort", Roberts insisted on reading his attack aloud to the company.

The abusive leaflet was published on 16th November, 1790; not content with this, Roberts had the whole correspondence reprinted in pamphlet form, "with his Remarks thereon, in Twelve Hundred Copies". In the preface he says that "the pamphlets are now selling by the booksellers; the profits Mr. Roberts has directed to be added to the Charity which is annually distributed by the Boroughreeve". As was pointed out later, Walker being that officer, "he was to be made not only the public, but the perpetual recorder of his own infamy".

Walker brought an action for libel against Roberts, which was heard at the Lancaster assizes on 28th March, 1791. Edward Law, the future Lord Ellenborough, was his counsel. Three years later Law was to be Walker's prosecutor on an infamous charge; but this time he did his job in the interests of justice sympathetically and efficiently, stressing the social harm that could spring from such venomous attacks—born of political hate and personal jealousy—being allowed to pass unpunished, and pointing out the great damage that such slander might do to the reputation of a well-known merchant and man of business.

Apart from the harm to him in his home town and all over England wherever he might have business connections, "this might travel beyond the limits of the realm". And what, asked Mr. Law, "is there to prevent any one who is the Enemy and Rival in Trade of Mr. Walker from sending it to every Foreign Country in which he has connexions and concerns? . . . Will any person say that if this libel was sent to Amsterdam, Francfort, Paris, Naples and many other places, it would not be intelligible to all of them?

"Or will any one assert that some man, envious of the prosperous and advancing fortune of the Gentleman near me, might not send that paper abroad, and thereby give effect to the malignant purpose of its original publisher?"

Mr. Law, "feeling it a question on which Mr. Walker's place and estimation in society—his domestic happiness and his REPUTATION which must be the foundation of both—most materially depend", urged the jury to "put the stamp of your reprobation upon this unprovoked attack, and make the Defendant feel, that the character of a Gentleman and a Merchant is not to be insulted in the County of Lancaster, without making ample reparation for such an injury".

The Judge concurred: "That this is a libel there can be no doubt"—and told the Jury to give the Plaintiff a retribution in damages. The verdict was the award of One Hundred Pounds Damages to be paid by Roberts.[1]

Walker saw to it that the trial was taken down in short-hand and the report published. In the *Mercury* for 23rd August, 1791, the "whole proceedings on the Trial for Libel" were advertised. Underneath the notice, Roberts, his hatred unquenched, had got the Tory editor to print an advertisement of his last attempt at defamation: "Supplementary Facts and Observations occasioned by Mr. Walker's Publication of his Prosecution of Mr. Roberts, with notes etc, price 3d." The notice adds that "it is printed on Paper the same size with the Trial and those who are in Possession of that are earnestly requested to annex this to it". The printer, J. Harrop, is "directed to give the Profits to the Charity for Poor Lying-in Women".

It seems that Roberts was optimistic enough to imagine he had by this had the last word. Although he had lost his case and £100 into the bargain (not to mention his voluminous printing expenses) he did not realise he had been defeated and made a laughingstock, nor that Walker's standing was too high to be seriously affected by his pinpricks.

The episode did Thomas Walker no real harm, though it caused him a certain amount of trouble and annoyance. In the light of later events, however, it could be seen as a sign of the spite and resentment that existed against him among a small but dangerous minority in the town. Dangerous, because it included the influential publisher, Harrop, and some others

---

[1] Verbatim report, *A Trial for Libel*, 1791.

with connections in high places—men who would go to almost
any lengths to damage the Radical merchant.

Thomas might have taken the affair as a warning to follow
counsels of compromise and prudence, had he been that sort of
person. But for better or worse, he was not that sort. He did
not care what Roberts and his like thought of him, as he had the
moral support of men he admired and respected to compensate
him; according to James Watt, writing to his father (10th
November, 1791) about the "Revolution Dinner" in London,
attended by many eminent men, Walker had been "unanimously elected Chairman, and received great applause at his
entering the Room—an honour which his exertions in favour
of the people entitle him to, and which must be doubly grateful
to him after his late disagreeable affair with Roberts, as it shows
a decided approbation for his Conduct in men no wise con-
nected with him . . .".[1]

Fortified by this approbation, Walker put past unpleasant-
ness behind him and went on his way.

[1] James Watt, jr., correspondence with his father.

## CHAPTER VI

## SOME EFFECTS OF THE FRENCH
## REVOLUTION (1791)

ONE of Walker's many public appearances during his term of office as Boroughreeve was as chairman at a meeting at the Exchange on 19th April, 1791, "for the purpose of considering the present alarming state of affairs between this country and Russia".

It should be explained that relations between Britain and Russia were somewhat strained at this time owing to what was termed "the Empress Catherine's views of aggrandizement" in the territory between the Dniester and Bug. Russia had annexed from the Turks a very considerable tract of country in that area, including the town of Oczakow, and refused to give it up.

The *Porte* was pressing for its return, and was supported by Prussia. Ever anxious to preserve the balance of power in Europe, Pitt's government stated to Parliament that we had a direct interest in any war between Russia and the *Porte*, and were under the necessity of arming, to give greater weight to our representations.

Fox and his group vehemently denied that our interests were endangered by the Russian advance in Turkey, and said that we should be satisfied with Catherine's withdrawal of her forces from the greater part of the territory she had taken. Followers of Fox, including Walker and his friends, campaigned vigorously in support of a peace policy, and sent up petitions and resolutions to Parliament, voicing their feelings.

At the meeting of 19th April, the first resolution that was passed declared that "the people of Britain should consider the evils of an impending war". The second was "that in the opinion of this meeting no nation can be justified in engaging in war unless for reasons and upon principles strictly defensive".

Further resolutions were to the effect that Great Britain, loaded as she was with heavy taxes and an enormous debt, should not engage in any war unless upon the most urgent and evident necessity. The people of the country who would be taxed to pay for it had a right to full and correct information of the reason for war. The meeting felt that no sufficient reason had been shown for a war with Russia . . . it was the people's representatives' duty (in Parliament) to refuse to allow extra burdens on the people till the expediency should be fully shown.

The war with Russia did not materialise. Walker thought this largely due to the popular protests; he and his supporters were delighted that these, and the wiser counsels of Fox, had prevailed; as their advocate, however, he was ferociously attacked in certain quarters for having ventured such opinions, and it even appeared that he might incur liability in publishing them. However, on consulting various experts his mind was set at rest on this: Mr. Sergeant Adair could see nothing illegal in the resolutions Walker had signed; nor could Thomas Lloyd, a young American lawyer of progressive ideas who was also consulted, along with Thomas Cooper, who was as able at the law as he was at chemistry. They all agreed that "it would be strange indeed if the Commons of England are not permitted to advise their representatives upon that subject of taxes, which, of all others, it is the peculiar business of the House of Commons to consider".

Nevertheless, Walker did not forget the attacks on him for having spoken his mind; though isolated, they brought home to him the fact that he was a marked man—first for identifying himself with the cause of civil and religious freedom; now for advocating peace instead of war. About this time, too, his boys were shouted at by their school-fellows: "There go Jacobin Walker's sons!"[1] The shame or annoyance that it caused them was probably more of a trial to Thomas than attacks on himself; but there was nothing to be done except to disregard opposition, and go on working for the causes which he thought just.

One occasion which he would on no account have missed, was the anniversary dinner of the French Revolution, on 14th July, 1791, organised by the Constitutional Society. This year, for the first time, it looked as if there might be trouble from the

[1] Jerrold, op. cit., p. 8.

opponents of the new government in France. When advertising
the dinner, the society requested "the Friends of Freedom to
take Precautions which very base and unmanly insinuations
had rendered necessary". It was hoped "that no Gentleman
will on that day move or introduce for discussion any question
relating to the political parties or local concerns of this country;
or wear any cockade or other badge of distinction, which may
give unnecessary offence to those of our fellow citizens who
have not yet been led to feel as ardently upon this great event as
ourselves . . . ".

Walker writes that "we wished peace and harmony to prevail
on all sides, and to leave opinions to find their own value. Not
so our adversaries; for on the morning before this, a most inflammatory hand-bill was distributed throughout the town,
containing amongst others this sentence—that 'if Englishmen
had the spirit they used to have, they would, on the 14th of
July, pull the house we assembled at over our heads; and the
brains of every man who dined there would much be improved
by being mingled with brick and mortar'."[1]

In Birmingham that day a dinner of the same kind was
taking place. It was to result in wild rioting by a mob, egged
on by the Radicals' enemies, against well-known Dissenters and
democrats. Dr. Joseph Priestley, the distinguished scientist and
Unitarian minister (who had incurred Church-and-King hatred
through his hard-hitting pamphlets, and the fact that he was a
prominent member of the rationalist Lunar Society) was the
worst sufferer, for his laboratory, his valuable equipment, and
his irreplaceable papers were destroyed. Matthew Boulton
escaped thanks only to the fact that his home and works were
on the other side of the town. The damage done to other
progressive citizens is described in a letter from Birmingham in
the *Manchester Mercury* on 17th July, which must have been read
with dismay by Walker and his friends:

"This town", said the reporter, "is in the greatest confusion
from a riot that has prevailed here in consequence of the cele-
bration of the French Revolution on Thursday last. The mischief already done is estimated at £150,000. The two Meeting
Houses of the Protestant Dissenters are entirely burnt down, as

[1] Walker, *Review*, pp. 22-3.

are the houses of Dr. Priestley, Mr. Humphreys, Mr. Hunt [and others]. . . .

"Indeed so far did the resentment of the mob carry them, that they burned a house occupied by Lady Carhampton because it belonged to Mr. Taylor. Upwards of a hundred lives have been lost, and most of the principal Inhabitants of the Town and Neighbourhood have left their Residences." The *Mercury* adds that "since the above was received a gentleman is arrived in the Birmingham Coach, who confirms the same with this addition, that there were fifteen Houses and Meeting Houses destroyed; that three Troops of the Oxford Blues were now within a mile of the Town, and it was not doubted but Peace and Tranquillity would soon be restored".

The editorial comment, heavily underlined, was: "*These are the dreadfull Effects of French Revolution Dinners.*"

A subsequent paragraph facetiously described A PAIR OF PICTURES recommended to be hung in the Dining-Room for such celebrations:

"ENGLAND—the King and People—United and Happy;
    FRANCE—the King a Prisoner—the People without a Head."

It was later known for certain that the riots were instigated by the Church and King party, who had agents among the crowd; that seditious papers had been placed among Priestley's affairs so as to incriminate him; that the authorities knew what was afoot but made no attempt to intervene—constables were nowhere to be found, and the troops were not called on till much too late.

When, eventually the rioters were tried, a packed and kindly-disposed jury let most of them off with a caution, while the chief sufferers were quite inadequately compensated (Priestley got only £2,000 instead of the £4,000 he had claimed).

Farther from the scene there was discreet satisfaction among certain political circles: "I am not sorry", wrote the Marquess of Buckingham; "Priestley's character justified anything . . .".[1]

The Lord Advocate of Scotland hoped that Edinburgh would serve its Unitarians the same way, and was "sure it would be

[1] Langford, *A Century of Birmingham Life*. Brown, *The French Revolution in English History*, p. 81.

winked at".[1] King George himself, while deploring the means used, none the less wrote to Dundas, his Home Secretary: "I cannot but feel better pleased that Priestley is the sufferer for the doctrines he and his party have instilled."[2]

However, although Priestley's losses and subsequent exile were hailed as a victory by the reactionaries, decent opinion in England was horrified when the doctor's own account of the riots appeared. For Radicals and Dissenters it was an ominous picture of what might happen to any of them if they relied on the protection of Tory authorities.

Walker wrote after the Manchester Dinner, that he had been "somewhat surprised that nothing of the same kind was attempted with us. But the state of things was not favourable to such an attempt at that season. . . . I had in a considerable degree the police of the town in my own hands as Borough-reeve, and most probably could have prevented any mischief by timely exertion.

"This was well known. The scheme, therefore, if any was in contemplation, proved abortive, and the day passed over in the utmost tranquility. But from the experience of what the unhappy families at Birmingham suffered . . . and from the symptoms of a persecuting spirit in the town of Manchester . . . I determined to be upon my guard, if any occurrence of a similar nature should ever take place here."[3]

Reading this passage in the light of what did take place in Manchester later on, one can only be thankful for Walker's sake that he was a shrewd and far-sighted man. In the meantime, he and his friends were allowed a breathing-space to carry on their activities. One of their good turns was a gift to Dr. Priestley "towards his indemnification on account of the riot in Birmingham". Priestley sent a letter of thanks to Walker, saying that "as a sufferer in the cause of liberty, I hope I am justified in accepting your very generous contribution . . . and I return you my grateful acknowledgments for it. Your address is too flattering to me. It will however be a motive with me to continue my experiments whatever they have been, in favour of truth and science, which, in thus patronising me, you wish to

[1] Lang MSS., No. 294, quoted Brown, p. 81.
[2] Langford, op. cit., i, p. 477.          [3] Walker, *Review*, pp. 23-4.

promote. And notwithstanding my losses, I consider myself as more than compensated by your testimony in my favour and that of others whose approbation I most value. Permit me to make my more particular acknowledgments to the member of the Church of England who joined in this contribution. Such liberality does honour to any religion, and certainly the rioters of Birmingham ought not to be considered as belonging to any church whatever."[1]

In spite of the riots, 1791 was a year of advance and hope for the progressives up and down the country. The French government was establishing itself, its constitutional methods winning even the Tories' grudging recognition. Burke was virtually the only prominent statesman publicly to attack the government in Paris and its supporters in England—which he did notably in his *Reflections on the French Revolution*, a direct onslaught on the distinguished Unitarian, Dr. Price, who had praised it in a sermon during November, 1789.

Burke's book at last roused the supporters of the *status quo* to a realisation that there were potential dangers for them in the establishment of the new order in France; his defence of the King and his abuse of the republicans became a banner round which a fierce battle was to rage; his phrase "the swinish multitude" was used with relish on both sides, seriously by his allies, satirically by his opponents.

While the *Reflections* were being read and discussed by everyone interested in politics, Radicals and Dissenters spoke out in defence of the Revolution; there were thirty-eight answers to Burke, the most famous being those of Paine, Mackintosh and Mary Wollstonecraft. Thomas Paine's book, *The Rights of Man*, in particular caused something of a sensation. It must have made much the same impression on the English Radicals as St. Paul's epistles made on the early Christians. Thomas Cooper was typical in his enthusiasm; he wrote to young Watt, in 1792, that "it has made me still more politically mad than I ever was.

"It is choque full, crowded with good sense and demonstrative reasoning, heightened also with a profusion of libellous matter.

"I regard it as the very jewel of a book . . . Burke is done

[1] Jerrold, op. cit., p. 40.

up for ever and ever by it—but Paine attacking Burke is dashing out the brains of a Butterfly with the Club of Hercules!" He admonishes his friend to "talk of it everywhere, read it as soon as you can get it, then get it by heart and retail it".

All over the country the book was eagerly read and passed round, especially among the members of the popular societies, who were delighted that Paine was putting their longings and ideals into words—and such vivid, evocative words.

When the second part of the *Rights of Man* appeared, Walker signed a Letter on behalf of the Manchester Society, congratulating the author. Paine replied in a cordial letter that "as we are all fellow labourers for the general happiness of the World I will not trouble the Society nor yourself with effusions of ceremonial gratitude. . . . As I am happy in any endeavour to do good, I feel that happiness increased by the approbation which the Society of Manchester has given me. . . ." He signed himself, "with much affection and regard, Your sincere and much obliged friend".

Another letter from Paine, to his "sincere friend" Walker, some months later, tells him that "the first and second parts of the *Rights of Man* are printing compleat and not in extract. They will come at ninepence each. The letter on the Convention will contain full as much matter as Mr. Macauly's halfcrown Answr to Mr. Burke, it will be printed close, and come at 6d on the same size paper as the *Rights of Man*. As we have now got the stone to roll, it must be kept going by cheap publications. This will embarass the Court gentry more than anything else, because it is a ground they are not used to."[1]

Thanks to Paine, and many minor pamphleteers, understanding of the political and social problems, and of how to solve some of them, grew and spread among the middle class, and more especially among the literate section of the working class. There was a lively desire to learn about events in France and their significance; and this was looked upon with deep misgiving by the reactionaries, as Walker points out:

"To the Manchester Society", he writes, "their adversaries imputed as a political offence never to be forgiven, that they approved of the French revolution, and the then constitution of

[1] Jerrold, op. cit., p. 41.

that country; ... in the affairs of France, we saw, as we thought, the most perfect and yet the most peaceful revolution to be found in the history of mankind. ... Was it criminal to look with delight and admiration on the prospect before us of so many millions of men ... restored to their rights from a condition of abject slavery?"[1]

Walker observes that France appeared to have acquired a state of freedom equal to that of America, but without the same struggle. At the Confederation of Paris, 14th July, 1790, the King, the Army and the great body of the people, accepted and ratified the Constitution.—"On July 14th 1791, the same ceremony took place, and the same harmony (notwithstanding the King's flight in June) appeared between him and the people." Where was violence or anarchy? Yet, popular sympathy towards the French people was advanced by the true-blues "as a proof of our designs to overturn the constitution of our own country, and to introduce a state of anarchy and confusion".

There was no evidence, let alone a proof, that the popular societies were aiming at or working for revolution in England. Though greatly encouraged by what had happened across the Channel, and while welcoming the new régime there as a prop for liberal ideas everywhere, the English Jacobins' objective was popular enlightenment and parliamentary reform, as they repeatedly proclaimed.

As we have noticed, however, the idea of reform had, through the French Revolution, been given a new lease of life in England, and a new significance.

A thorough overhaul of the electoral system had been mooted as an important issue in the years following the American war, when Major John Cartwright (no revolutionary, though a person of great independence of mind, and a good friend of Thomas Walker's) had launched his campaign throughout the country. In those days it had been so safe and respectable that among its adherents were Pitt, Burke, the Duke of Richmond, and many others of the ruling class.

The period of the unchallenged supremacy of a small group of aristocrats was ending; and though the *status quo* was acceptable and unashamedly accepted by the well-to-do, certain

[1] Walker, *Review*, pp. 18-21.

E

sections of the upper classes who were outside the privileged circles of court and ministry favoured a movement which would give them a bigger share of power. Many manufacturers and even members of the squirearchy disapproved of the unequal representation in Parliament and of the existing system of corruption and graft and pensions, and they were willing to support electoral changes which would give them more say in the country's affairs.

The methods of election were indeed shocking: they included absurd anachronisms which resulted in a majority of seats going to a group of very wealthy landowners and Tory churchmen: for instance, Dissenters were excluded because of the seventeenth century Test Acts, which had never been justified, but were less than ever applicable; Catholics were debarred even from voting, because they had once been accounted traitors; important growing towns such as Manchester, Sheffield and Liverpool might not send members to Parliament because they had recently been villages; while villages might send two members, because they had once been towns. Cornwall, owing to royal influence in bygone days, had a representation equal to the whole of Scotland.

Equally unfair was the method by which seats were bought and sold. One candid aristocrat remarked on one occasion that "the price of a seat in Parliament is better known than the price of a horse". It was, in fact, well known to be anything over £2,000.

And although a certain number of members were honestly elected and tried seriously to represent their constituents, the fact that about half the House of Commons (254 members) were put there by only 6,000 people, was in itself an indictment of the representation.

However, parliamentary reform could not become a reality except by fairly drastic methods, entailing united pressure at all levels; it could not be achieved simply by voting, as the Houses were packed with pensioners and members of the privileged circle who would certainly not vote themselves out of their comfortable seats. Cartwright's campaign was doomed to failure in spite of intensive activity, for it had no mass backing. Pitt brought a bill for reform before the Commons in May,

1782, and again in April, 1783, and yet again in May, 1785—with the support of the influential "Westminster Committee"—and was defeated every time.

But with the revival of activity in 1791, Reform had quite a different look about it. The populations of the industrial centres were far more important now, and conscious of their strength and significance. Reform no longer meant a more equal sharing of the cake of influence among the upper classes—it held a promise of a better life for the underdog, and the achievement of this was the purpose of the popular societies, which they honestly hoped to arrive at by peaceful and constitional means.

A "Letter to the Reforming Societies in Sheffield" (reprinted in two thousand copies by the Manchester Society), gives a fair picture of the attitude of the reformers throughout this period. The writer exhorts his readers to "promote with firmness, by all just, legal and peaceable means, a Reform in the Representation of the People; maintain the Freedom of the Press—that indispensable safeguard to your liberties—and assert in the like calm and peaceable way, your right to free discussion on political subjects . . .".

Political Reform, we are told, will be a safeguard against oppression, and "produce more general comfort and happiness".

The letter urges "the necessity of letting personal amendment go hand in hand with Political Reform and Information. . . . From your general behaviour let no one be able to point out a Reformer or a member of one of your Societies, without at the same time he shall point to an industrious, regular man of sober manners, and an orderly peaceable disposition."

"By being meritorious servants, good masters, kind husbands, and provident fathers, you will put yourselves on an equality with men in higher stations and but too frequently become their superiors in real worth and usefulness. . . ."[1]

The writer might have added to his list the virtues of generosity, courage and endurance. As we shall see, these were the most necessary of all, and luckily many of the reformers—at any rate the Manchester Radicals—possessed them in good measure.

[1] Appendix to Walker Trial.

## CHAPTER VII

## RADICAL ACTIVITY (1792, Spring)

THE spring of 1792 brought a change for the worse in the political atmosphere. The government began to wake up to the implications of the widespread popular interest in France (as well as to the significance of the French Revolution itself), and to consider how that interest could be checked. At the same time there came an event which was to be of great importance in stimulating the "democratic" movement, and which was wholeheartedly welcomed by the existing popular societies. This was the formation, on 20th January, of the London Corresponding Society, based on the support of working men in London; it was to satisfy an urgent need in linking up by correspondence all the other societies.

The L.C.S. (as we will call it for brevity's sake) was the first central organisation really to represent the working people. There were other groups: the "Constitutional Society" (Society for Constitutional Information), led by eminent middle-class reformers, for middle-class members; and the organisation known as the "Friends of the People", whose leaders considered themselves the *élite*, disclaimed any sympathy with the French Revolution, and shied away from anything savouring of Republicanism. This group declined to correspond even with the "temperate" Constitutional Society, because the latter approved of Paine; and attempts were made at one stage to get rid of even the respectable Major Cartwright from its ranks.

The Friends of the People served a useful purpose in a limited way (chiefly in bringing pressure through its M.P. supporters on Parliament), but its importance and influence were not comparable with those of the other two groups, and its constant compromises resulted eventually in self-extinction.

The L.C.S., on the contrary, was a very lively organisation and full of fight. It was fortunate in being blessed with a most intelligent, energetic and devoted secretary, Thomas Hardy, a shoemaker who lived and cobbled in Piccadilly. He had the valuable support of John Horne Tooke—eminent free-lance politician and philologist, famous conversationalist—"a keen iron man" as Coleridge called him; of Felix Vaughan, Tooke's nephew, a brilliant lawyer; of Thomas Lloyd, a young American, also a clever lawyer; of John Frost, Maurice Margarot, Thomas Holcroft, and other able professional men. They helped in an intellectual capacity very actively indeed, providing ideas, writing pamphlets and manifestoes, speaking at meetings, and so on; but Hardy's is the credit for actually having made the society succeed. He was responsible for the functioning of its London divisions (consisting of up to sixty members each, with a penny a week subscription), and for organising meetings all over the city, sending resolutions to Parliament, preparing publications, and so forth. He also carried on single-handed the voluminous correspondence with societies all over the country including Derby, Newcastle, Bath, Norwich, Manchester, to mention only a few.

The Manchester Society had been in touch with the lately revived Constitutional Information Society, which besides Horne Tooke and Cartwright included as members Thomas Paine, Rickman the bookseller, William Sharp the engraver, and other celebrities, and held dinners to which the leading Radicals from the provinces were invited. Walker was often present at these dinners, as guest or steward, or wrote regretfully excusing himself. But it was clear that the L.C.S. was going to serve a more useful purpose, and the Mancunians heartily concurred with Hardy's initial letter to Walker expressing a wish "to enter into correspondence and be in close connexion with you. . . . As we are all engaged in one common cause our sentiments ought to be known to each other and act with one heart in a matter of such vast importance."[1]

The aims of the two societies were very much the same; yet however much they might protest their peaceful intentions and limited objectives, for Pitt's government the fact that they were (a) sympathetic to the French Revolution, (b) in correspondence with each other, was enough pretext to accuse them of seditious and violent intentions. The men of property were becoming more and more uneasy as the progressive movement spread.

[1] Treasury Solicitor's Papers, 3505.

Although Britain was not yet at war with France, the political situation was quite different from that of 1782 and 1783 when reform had been a perfectly respectable plaything for politicians in opposition. Burke's *Reflections* and Paine's *Rights of Man* had each in its own way frightened the authorities into accepting the idea of repression. And once the idea had taken hold, it was difficult to prevent it spreading and running wild, as the easy-going people of England later found to their cost.

It had become evident some time previously that the scales were being weighted against the Radicals by pressure from high places. Walker and his friends felt it when they tried to get articles or advertisements into the local Press, as we learn from a letter of Thomas Cooper's, written "from Mr. Walker's confined by illness to my bed", to Horne Tooke, in August, 1791.

Tooke had sent him a pro-French article for publication in the Manchester press; Walker had taken it to Charles Wheeler, the owner of the more moderate of the two local papers, but had had a reply complaining that the address was "abounding with objectionable remarks for publication, remarks which have a right to subject both the author and publisher to a prosecution".

Wheeler, while admitting that "it may be said that Government will not prosecute for such publication", said "that does not lessen the *Folly* of the Publisher in running a Risque which it is his *Duty* as a member of Society to avoid"; "he cannot but declare that he would wish in future to avoid publishing what may hold out improper ideas to the public at large, who seldom *think* much before they *act*—of this there is a recent and melancholy instance". (Mr. Wheeler was probably thinking of the Birmingham riots.) He went on to say that he "is obliged to trouble Mr. Walker thus far in his own vindication; and he cannot help observing that it is with extreme regret that he is now, or may be at a future date, obliged to secede from any service which Mr. Walker may wish him to perform".

Cooper goes on to say that "in Manchester there are two papers published weekly; one of them most decidedly and virulently aristocrat. The other (Chas. Wheeler's) generally moderate and rather in our favour than adverse. But you see that now we are decidedly excluded from that, not only on occasion of your address but in every other future political subject. . . . We shall therefore immediately set up a paper among ourselves, which I have formerly mentioned to you, and which we have not hitherto done because we thought that Wheeler would have no objection on being paid, to insert what we thought fit.

"Can you lend us any and what assistance in point of Communication to such a Paper? it will *at first* be gently but always decidedly democratish, nor pestered with much presbyterian nonsense. Can you give us any hints about it? We have already spoken to Sharpe. . . ."

Cooper's last words in this letter show how Horne Tooke's opinion was sought and valued on all matters concerning books and publications. It also shows Tooke's slightly casual attitude towards his correspondents:

"I wrote to you about an intended abridgment of Paine— You sent me no answer of any kind—I wish you had, because I had a formal request from our Society here to publish it. The Preface I sent you with it, if you have, burn."[1]

There must have been a number of hitches before the new "democratish" paper got to the point of publication. Perhaps Horne Tooke delayed, or never bothered, to give an answer; perhaps it was difficult to collect the necessary subscriptions; whatever the reason, it was several months before the paper was born—but born it eventually was, and christened the *Manchester Herald*; Cooper was the editor, and Matthew Falkner and Samuel Birch its printers.

Its creators were surely pleased with their child. It was a good-sized four-page newspaper, with a very pleasant lay-out, excellent print, and varied contents. Its aims were stated in the leading article of one of its first numbers, on Saturday, 31st March, 1792:

"To the Public.—That there is ample room for the publication of another Newspaper in Manchester, those who have attended to the rapid increase of its Commerce and Population will readily allow. That there is merit in the Conduct of those papers already published we chearfully admit. . . . But *different* Editors have *different* modes of instructing and amusing their readers."

[1] Treasury Solicitor's Papers, 3505.

The paper claimed "to have more ample sources of intelligence than usually fall to the share of the conductors of a Provincial Paper . . ." but "we shall spare little room for articles of *fashionable* intent—for accounts of Court Dresses or Court Intrigues—of Hunting Parties, Drinking Parties or Visiting Parties—interesting only to the Butterflies of Society . . .". Still less, said the Editors, "shall we defile our pages with prurient details of the vices and debaucheries of the fashionable world—almost equally disgraceful to those who thus wantonly narrate them—to the reader who greedily peruses them—and to the persons who thus shamefully commit them".

Omission of these items would leave room for accounts of Parliamentary debates, and important events. "The POLITICAL complexion . . . shall be neither ministerial nor anti-ministerial. . . . We shall not favour any cause but the *cause of the public*. We do not profess, nor will we exercise that lukewarm caution and prudent moderation which casts a veil over political delinquency, and conceals from the public *what the public ought to know*. We are aware of the dangerous and unconstitutional extent of the doctrine of LIBEL and we are not anxious to incur the lash of the law by indulging unnecessary freedom. But short of this no fear nor favour shall prevent us from making our publication *decidedly* the PAPER OF THE PEOPLE."

The newspaper was as good as its word, and throughout its fifty-odd issues there was nothing in the way of a gossip column nor sensation-mongering; it was definitely a paper for the serious-minded. But it had its lighter side, and, though it is difficult to estimate the circulation, it seems to have been well supported to judge by the number and variety of advertisements peppered all over its pages. They range from "genteel Lodgings" and Post-Chaises ("NEAT CHAISES, good horses, carefull drivers") to a Cure for Corns, or the "famous Parisian VEGETABLE SYRUP" (guaranteed to cure almost any complaint); you could find an Academy for your daughter, or learn of the sale of "two long-tailed Geldings by Auction", or—a reminder that this is Manchester—of "Best Superfine Clothes at Prime Cost— Scarlet Frizes, Cashmeres, Toilanettes, Swansdowns, Lasting, Fustian, Nankeens"; not to mention "a Variety of Silke

Florentines, Armazeens, Bombazeens, Morettas, Russelo, Wildbotes, Durants, and Blankets".

Progressive books and pamphlets were, of course, advertised regularly: one week "The following publications on the Slave Trade", the next "The French Constitution, by Benjamin Flower", the third "A second edition of the authentic account of the Riots in Birmingham".

Notices of the popular Societies and news of their activities are prominent in almost every number, and these give an idea of how deeply the "reformers" were involved in every progressive cause of the day. The abolition of the Slave Trade, a burning issue in 1792, was one of Thomas Walker's good causes, and in one number we read this announcement, signed by him as chairman of the Manchester Committee:

"SPENCER'S TAVERN, March 16th, 1792. 'At a general meeting of the subscribers in this place for effecting the Abolition of the Slave Trade . . . a Resolution to be transmitted to Wm Wilberforce . . . that the further sum of One Hundred Guineas be sent to the London Committees'."

On 23rd March a subscription list was published (Walker being down on it for £2 2s. 0d.) with an announcement of further meetings to be held "each Tuesday at 5 p.m.".

On 28th April, the editorial let fly at the unsatisfactory decision of Parliament to defer abolition: "Seven years longer is the infernal trade of Slavery, Rapine, Cruelty and Murder to exist. . . . With grief do we announce that the result [of the debate] was that the Slave Trade should be sanctioned till the year 1800. Humanity blushes at the decree—she *weeps indignant* while she announces to the world the tardiness of the representatives of the people of Britain to do justice. . . ."

The editor taunts Parliament in a paragraph on "Mr. Harry Gradual", and asks "for what purpose does Parliament assemble but to transact the business of the Nation?"

Among other notices in the *Manchester Herald*, those of the Constitutional Society's activities are frequent and prominent. The resolution of thanks to Thomas Paine for the second part of the *Rights of Man*, signed by Walker, appears on 31st March, and Paine's answer is printed the following week. The *Herald* acts, in fact, as a sort of diary of the life of the Radicals during this period, and we can trace all their doings through its pages. It gave, of course, a full account of the visit of the two Manchester delegates—Thomas Cooper and James Watt junior— to Paris, where they presented an address on behalf of their society to the Society of Jacobins; this was an event which sparked off a highly explosive train, and brought our friends nation-wide notoriety.

The address, to quote Walker, on 30th April "produced a most virulent invective from Mr. Burke, in the House of Commons. On the 8th of May the Manchester Society published translations of the Address and the Reply to it." Thomas Cooper wrote, in defence of the French and himself, a "Reply to Burke's Invective"—"A publication," says Walker, "which from the very favourable acceptance of the public was certainly worthy of an answer, but to which Mr. Burke has not yet condescended to reply, either from want of inclination, or more probably, from want of argument."

The Society became "the object of much conversation and calumny" and to prevent misrepresentation "the members thought it necessary . . . to publish the following declaration of their view and intentions".

This (published in the *Herald*) states "the political maxims in which individually and collectively we agree: That the power vested in every government is derived from the people; that the persons who exercise it are ultimately responsible to them; and that the happiness of the people should be the sole end of every government." The declaration disclaims "any intention of endeavouring to overthrow the British Constitution—our aim is to restore the constitution to its original purity, by removing the corruptions and abuses that deform it . . .".

Whoever drew up the declaration—probably Walker and Cooper—must have enjoyed quoting Mr. Burke on the subject of Reform, in February, 1780: "What I confess is uppermost with me . . . was the reduction of that corrupt influence which is itself the perennial spring of all prodigality and of all disorder." They must have smiled sardonically, recalling Burke's support of the motion adopted "not many years ago" in the House, "that the Influence of the Crown has increased, is increasing, and ought to be diminished"; and his appeal to

Parliament to "consider the wisdom of a timely reform".

After reminding the public of Burke's championship of their objectives, the authors of the manifesto vigorously defend their society against the charge of being a revolutionary or dangerous body: "Instead of endeavouring to excite sedition, we are solicitous, by a timely and well-directed reform of abuses, to remove all pretences for it. . . ."

As to their attitude towards the French Revolution, "we do not pledge ourselves to an approbation of all the measures . . . we most sincerely deplore any calamities . . . and would not insinuate that such a revolution as was made necessary by the wickedness of the former government of France is requisite for the very different circumstances of Great Britain". But they do express joy at the emancipation of the French people, and at the lofty aims of their government.

The declaration may have convinced the readers of the *Manchester Herald* of the society's good faith, but it did not, unfortunately, touch the hearts of the men in the ministries. The increasing contacts with France, the growing membership of the popular societies, and the number of new groups springing up all over the country, the widespread distribution of their leaflets and books, the thousandfold sales of the *Rights of Man* (issued now in a 6*d*. edition)—all threw the authorities into a state near panic, and added fuel to their determination to stop these goings-on, by whatever means.

A Royal Proclamation was published in the *London Gazette*, on Tuesday, 22nd May, 1792, declaring that "whereas divers wicked and seditious writings have been printed, published and industriously dispersed, tending to excite tumult and disorder, by endeavouring to raise groundless jealousies and discontents in the minds of our faithful and loving subjects . . . and whereas we have also reason to believe that correspondencies have been entered into with sundry persons in foreign parts, with a view to forward the criminal and wicked purposes above mentioned . . ." his Majesty "solemnly warned" his loving subjects "to guard against all such attempts which aim at the subversion of all regular government", and earnestly exhorted them "at all times to avoid and discourage all proceedings tending to produce riots and tumults".

"We do strictly charge and command all our magistrates," continues the Proclamation, "that they do make diligent enquiry, in order to discover the authors and printers of such wicked and seditious writings . . . ." All sheriffs, Justices of the Peace, officers and magistrates are ordered to join in suppressing riots and tumults, and magistrates are required to transmit to the secretaries of State "due and full information of such persons as shall be found offending as aforesaid".

One immediate effect of the Proclamation was exactly the opposite to that intended. Owing to the fact that at the very same moment Thomas Paine appeared before the King's Bench Court for a seditious libel (based on certain passages in the *Rights of Man*, part two) the sales of the book leapt to undreamed-of numbers; thanks to the free advertisement, one bookseller increased his sale from one copy to 750; and the estimate of a total circulation of 200,000, made the following year, is probable enough.

The sales of other "subversive" literature swelled; we read in the *Manchester Herald* that "a London bookseller lately sent down a few copies of *The Patriot* to Newcastle along with some advertisements which were posted in that town. The Mayor ordered the sergeants of the corporation to take them down or deface them. The consequence was the natural one—the curiosity of the public was aroused—the copies were not half sufficient to supply the town."

On the other hand, the Proclamation gave the word go to the Church and King clubs up and down the country. In Manchester it was hailed with jubilation by the Tories who called a meeting for 4th June (his Majesty's birthday) in its support.

The Constitutional Society issued a letter, signed by Thomas Walker and Samuel Jackson, protesting against the proposed meeting in particular and against the Proclamation in general.

"Hitherto," they wrote, "the people of England have supposed the statutes of this realm, duly executed, were sufficient of themselves to prevent or to punish offence against the state. . . ."

Up to now they imagined that "the peaceable discussion of the errors and abuses which time may have introduced into the constitution . . . was not only their privilege but their right . . .".

The proclamation, "so inadvisedly issued", found people "neither distrusting the laws of their country, nor involved in any riotous meetings or tumultuous discussions . . . the true friends of their country have been grieved to see this state of the public mind so materially disturbed by the late Proclamation— the obvious tendency of which is to create alarm where none existed before—to sow the seeds of mutual discord and suspicion . . . to excite distrust of the laws, the magistrates, and the government of the country—and to give existence to those very *proceedings tending to produce riot and tumult* which it professes to guard against".

As to the public meeting, "in the present agitated state of the public mind, the impropriety of such a meeting cannot be doubted"; and "the obvious tendency, of a multitude of people, of various and opposite sentiments assembling to discuss a public measure of a most violent nature, and containing the most dubious assertions, and the most personal allusions, is too glaring to be mistaken. . . . The cause of the people would inevitably be injured by violence and tumult. . . . This is the game for their enemies to play; and there is reason to believe the opportunities will be eagerly sought for."

The Society exhorted its members and friends to "evince themselves the true friends also of public peace and good order, by abstaining from the meeting of Monday next . . . which however upright the motives of the persons who have called it, has a direct tendency, *at the present crisis*, to endanger the harmony and tranquillity of the town and neighbourhood".

The *Herald*, which had protested vigorously against the Proclamation, published the Society's letter; it also published an advertisement of the true-blue meeting, and a curiously objective report of the events attending it.

"On Monday the Boroughreeve and Constables, very numerously and respectably attended, walked in procession to St. Anne's Square, where the Royal Scots Greys were drawn up and fired four excellent Vollies. On the same day there was a public dinner and in the evening a ball on the occasion."

According to Walker, although the meeting may have passed off quietly, "in the evening of Monday a considerable number

of people assembled in St. Ann's Square, to see some illumina-
tions exhibited by two of his Majesty's tradesmen, when the
crowd became very tumultuous, and assaulted several peaceable spectators; they proceeded to tear up several of the trees
growing there, one of which was carried with great triumph to
the Dissenters' Chapel, near the square, and the gates attempted
to be forced open, with violent cries of 'Church and King'—
'Down with the Rump—Down with it', etc., etc. . . .

"Another tree was carried in the same riotous manner, and
with the same exultations to the Unitarian chapel in Mosley-
Street; fortunately, however, the doors withstood the attacks
made upon them, the people were persuaded gradually to disperse, and about one o'clock in the morning the streets became
quiet without any further damage."[1]

To return to the source of all the trouble, the Royal Proclamation, there was no lack of stout champions of the writer
and of the Press, to attack the assault on civil liberties. In the
*Herald* of 2nd June, Thomas Cooper, under the pseudonym of
"Sydney", wrote that "the public have been not a little
surprized at the appearance of a proclamation, the most extraordinary perhaps that the annals of the country have produced,
and singularly well calculated to produce the alarm which it is
apparently meant to allay; by hints and insinuations . . . the
astonished reader is taught to expect some unknown evil, which
he attempts in vain to discover from the proclamation itself. . . .
Involved as it is in darkness and ambiguity, dealing in fears
without specifying the foundation, and creating suspicions
without removing them, each man is tempted to ask his neighbour 'Who are the persons? where are the meetings? which are
the writings?' The evil spirit of criminal conjecture is let loose
upon the public, by authority, to stab the reputation of the
innocent; and the malignant passions of private pique and
public prejudice have full play and ample gratification."

Cooper certainly echoes the questioning bewilderment of the
ordinary public, both in the preceding words, and in his last
query: "After all, why this general anxiety among ministers to
stop the progress of knowledge and cut off the sources of political information? Why this dread lest the people (the Swinish

[1] Walker, *Review*, pp. 34-7.

Multitude as their friend Mr. Burke calls them) should think too much and reason too much on their own rights and their own interests?"

Answer came there none—as might have been foreseen.

On 9th June a wag calling himself Marmaduke Meanwell wrote to the *Herald* in a lighter vein: he bemoaned the fact that "neither I nor my family have had any peace of mind since the appearance of the Proclamation. . . . Many honest folk, knowing that I had been educated at a Grammar School came to me to desire that I would inform them what *Sedition* was, for that they were sorely afraid of offending the Proclamation without any intention . . . Happily I chanced to remember what a publican once told me about the effects of fermentation in Porter and Ale . . . when the fermentation subsided the Sedition always went to the bottom, especially if you put a little Bullock's Blood in it. . . ."

Another humorist published a "Genealogy of Discontent" which ran thus: "Ministerial Ambition begat Corruption which begat State Necessity which begat Exaction which begat Discontent which begat an Alarm which begat an Encampment which begat a Proclamation which begat New Discontents. . . ."

As mentioned earlier, the Proclamation had the effect of stimulating loyalty and activity on both sides; on the one hand, new popular societies sprang into being—in Manchester the Patriotic Society (pledged "to gain by constitutional means a fair and adequate representation in Parliament") and the Reformation Society (also formed to co-operate with others for the purpose of obtaining a parliamentary reform).

They both emphasised their peaceable intentions: "the Arms of Reason are our only Weapons" said the former; and "we renounce and disclaim all riots and tumults", the latter.

Both were formed, in the main, of working men—weavers, labourers and journeymen; whereas the Constitutional Society consisted chiefly of progressive "gentlemen".

On the other hand, according to Walker, "The High Churchmen were not behind in their professions of loyalty . . .". The "Tythe and Tax Club" judged this an opportune moment to publish their principles in an address which abounded in purple patches. "This Society," it goes, "beholds with infinite concern the many dangerous plots and associations that are forming . . . for the avowed purpose of disseminating discord and for subverting the order of one of the most beautiful systems of government that the combined efforts of human wisdom has ever yet been able to accomplish. . . .

"When we see such *deadly wounds* aimed at our glorious constitution we consider it the duty of all good citizens publicly to step forward and express their abhorrence of the malevolent and most wicked intentions of those disappointed men, who are audaciously clamorous for a reform in parliament, but whose real object is to excite civil commotion in this our *happy* and well-governed state. We are far from believing should they ever effect their purpose (which God forbid!) that the change would be for the better, but must always regard those persons as the bane of civil society. . . ."

This "Address" must have been typical of what was being vociferated by government supporters all over the country, and so must its "declaration of principles", among which are "reprobation of the wild theories and seditious doctrines respecting the Rights of Man", the opinion "that the Corporation and Test Acts are the great Bulwark of our Constitution and therefore ought never to be repealed", and so on.

As Walker says, the meetings called to air these sentiments "in almost every part of the kingdom" had a disastrous effect; under pretence of stimulating patriotism and loyalty, "all the bad passions of party were let loose, and political rancour against the friends of *reform* became a virtue of the first magnitude".[1]

These passions and rancour became a habit and the foundation of a legalising of repression which was to ruin many a good and honest man merely because he was a political or religious dissenter. The Proclamation was the source of the trickle which was to become a mighty—and a very muddy—torrent, flooding across England, sullying her fair name, and sweeping away some of her best citizens' rights, reputations, liberties and livelihoods.

[1] Walker, *Review*, pp. 34-7.

## CHAPTER VIII

## REPRESSION (1792, Autumn)

BY the late summer of 1792 the young French Republic
was running into heavy seas. Hitherto the Republicans
had behaved strictly legally, the King had kept his
position, if not his former prestige, the new constitution, peace-
fully voted in, was being implemented in as orderly a manner as
was possible, and there had been no reason to suppose that the
revolution would not be consolidated without any further
upheaval. Unfortunately this was not to be; the emigré aristocrats had been conspiring with their opposite numbers in
Austria and Germany, and the young Republic found itself
faced with an aggressive enemy outside as well as within its
frontiers.

The Terror, unleashed as a result of popular fury and
indignation at the conspiracy, was given much lurid publicity
by the British government and the Press which did not explain
the reasons for the atrocities, but played on the kind nature
of the English to work up horror and fear of the French.

But there were not a few English men and women who
understood what was responsible for the September massacres:
Walker asks in his Review: "Which of these calamities took
place before the concert of Princes; before the treaty of Pilnitz;
before the well-known Manifesto by the Duke of Brunswick,
on the part of our *faithful* ally his Majesty of Prussia; before
the *actual invasion* of France by the Continental Despots; and,
finally, before the *treacherous* surrender of some important
fortresses into their hands?"[1]

Though deploring the terror, most British Radicals sym-
pathised strongly with the invaded French, and began, from the
outbreak of the fighting, to collect money and clothing for the
*sans-culottes*. By November we learn that the Constitutional
Information Society had collected over £780.

[1] Walker, *Review*, p. 22.

F

Subscription lists were published at intervals; one such list, published on 30th November, of subscriptions "for the purpose of assisting the efforts of France in the Cause of Freedom", shows the variety of people who supported the fund:

| | |
|---|---|
| John Richards, gunmaker . . . | £1  5s. 6d. |
| Captain Ryder Mowat. One days' half pay | 5s. 0d. |
| Thomas Lloyd (an American Lawyer) . | £2  11s. 6d. |

and anonymous donors:

"A Fig for the Duke of Brunswick"  .  . £1  5s. 6d. and "For the Brave French People—Five Days' Pay."[1]

The Manchester Constitutional Society was not behind with its gesture of solidarity: as early as 12th September, the *Herald* published its proposal to meet at the Bull's Head, "to set on foot a subscription for the relief of our brethren in France, who are at present suffering all the calamities of war, in consequence of a most cruel combination of despots, against the dawning liberty of that country, and which may eventually be employed . . . to the destruction of our own".

This would appear a harmless enough proceeding, and it could hardly be a cause of grievance to the owners of the public houses which were the only meeting grounds of the popular societies, and which had from time immemorial been open to any citizen who drank his cup and paid his bill.

However it provided the much-needed pretext for which the enemies of the reformers had been waiting. Tories high up in the local administration had been working on the innkeepers for some time past, so Walker tells us:

"A few months after [the Proclamation] a tax-gatherer and some other persons, went round the town of Manchester to all the innkeepers and publicans, advising them as they valued themselves, to suffer no societies similar to ours . . . to meet at their houses. The publicans thought their licenses of more value than our custom, and would receive neither the Constitutional, the Patriotic nor the Reformation societies any longer. . . . In thus acting they probably consulted their interest, but the mode

[1] Treasury Solicitor's Papers, 3495.

of their doing it was too descriptive of the temper of the high church party at that time to be omitted."

On 13th September, 1792, 186 innkeepers and alehouse keepers issued a declaration, expressing themselves "justly alarmed at the *treasonable and seditious* conduct of a well-known set of daring MISCREANTS, who have called a public meeting, for the avowed purpose of assisting the French Savages". They stressed their "detestation of such wicked and abominable PRACTICES", and solemnly declared "that we will *not suffer* any meeting to be held in our houses, of any CLUBS or societies, however specious or plausible their titles may be, that have a tendency to put in force what those INFERNALS SO *ardently* and *devoutly wish for*, namely the DESTRUCTION of this COUNTRY, and *we* will be ready on all occasions to co-operate with our fellow-townsmen in *bringing to justice* all those who shall offend in any instance against our MUCH-ADMIRED AND MOST EXCELLENT CONSTITUTION".[1]

The members of the Church and King Club must indeed have rubbed their hands when this declaration appeared in the Press. To have won the co-operation of 186 innkeepers was something of a triumph; and we are led to believe that the number was even greater, from a satirical item in the *Manchester Herald* in September.

"Sir," writes the humorist, "I wish very much to become the universal applauder of the 228 virtuous and loyal innkeepers and publicans in general of the towns of Manchester and Salford, as they are stiled in Mr. Harrop's of September 27th." He says he is "at a loss to determine which is the most worthy of admiration and applause, the immaculate modesty of these political bonnifaces in obtruding themselves on the notice of the public, or the very neat well turned periods and elegant phrases which compose their advertisements.

"I cannot however desist from congratulating Manchester on possessing so great a number of men of their astonishing erudition and constitutional knowledge, and please myself with the idea that when I visit Manchester I shall have no occasion to be afraid of being accounted seditious.

"I have never been in an alehouse since I wrote to you before,

[1] Walker, *Review*, pp. 41-4.

and I long to go to Manchester, for there, I find, I can visit every sot's hole without the smallest danger of being suspected." However he expresses some anxiety on one point: "Pray, Mr. Printer, do you think all these innkeepers examine travellers the moment they get off their horses, to know what they think of the times and all that sort of thing? . . . We strangers should know this, for if they should discover one was inwardly inclined to wish well to the poor French, they might turn one out into the open air at midnight. . . ."

Whatever the fate of this correspondent at the hands of the innkeepers, that of the Constitutional Society was obvious enough. Walker writes, that "the society having now no regular place of meeting . . . I offered them the use of my house at Manchester until they could accommodate themselves elsewhere. As I mostly resided five miles from Manchester in a house which I then rented at Barlow, it caused no interruption or inconvenience to myself or my family. The high church party having thus failed of routing the jacobins (as the friends of civil and religious liberty were now termed all over Europe) their animosity was principally directed against me for having furnished the place of meeting for the society to which I belonged."

Walker's act was particularly courageous, as he had a shrewd suspicion that he and his property were a target for the reactionaries of the town, and that they wanted no encouragement to damage him. As early as January, 1792 he had had a warning from his landlord, Mr. Egerton, the Tory M.P. for Newcastle in Staffordshire, in the course of the following conversation:

MR. EGERTON. I have been very uneasy, and my uneasiness has prevented me from sooner coming to Barlow. . . . From the decisive part which you have taken in public affairs, I have been very much afraid that your house would have been pulled down.

MR. WALKER. Sir!

MR. E. I mean *my* house.

MR. W. I am really at a loss to know what you mean.

MR. E. I think it right to be explicit, and to say that I have been very apprehensive from the part you have taken, that my house would have been pulled down. *In fact, I know it was intended to pull your houses down.*

MR. W. To me you appear much mistaken, for I think the people begin to know better than to treat their real friends in the manner you seem to insinuate. But . . . if you expect I should regulate my opinions by yours, you will be very much mistaken. The part I have taken I have not adopted without mature deliberation, and without being perfectly convinced it is right. I will not therefore suffer any man to dictate to me.

MR. E. I do not expect it, but my property is in danger.

MR. W. While I live in your house I shall not permit it easily to be pulled down, as independently of my property, I have a very great stake in it, my wife and six children.

MR. E. Sir, property is everything to me.[1]

How nearly Mr. Egerton's premonitions came into effect is another chapter. Meanwhile, the innkeepers' declaration of September was the beginning of an intensification of propaganda against the reformers and all their sympathisers. As the events in France became more serious, the authorities, in London and locally, used them to work up feeling against friends of the French Republic, in England.

The fate of the French nobility, the distribution of land to the peasants, was what chiefly frightened the British ruling class (who were themselves predominantly members of the landed aristocracy). Henry Dundas, Home Secretary, visiting Scotland that autumn, reported that "the lower ranks" had been "poisoned with an enthusiastic rage for liberty that will not be crushed without coercive measures".[2]

In Manchester, despite all attempts to check the popular societies, activity was increasing. On 6th October, 1792, Thomas Cooper wrote to James Watt junior that "we are going on here much as you may expect . . . advancing slowly and in the midst of much obliquy—but I hope quietly and surely. The Cause is good and worthy every exertion that common Prudence will possibly allow. . . ." Thomas Walker, writing about the same time, denies some gloomy forecasts of

---

[1] Walker, *Review*, p. 44.    [2] Brown, op. cit., p. 94.

Horne Tooke's: "nothing could be more erroneous; the justice of our cause and the *fears* of our adversaries leave us everything to hope". The collections for the French have gone ahead in spite of obstacles, and Walker says "our subscription will either be sent in the mode you put out, or to the National Convention to be distributed by them to the Orphans and Widows of our excellent Citizen Brethren who have fallen in the defence of the Liberties of Mankind . . .".

As for the popular societies, they were active and growing steadily. The Constitutional Society was meeting regularly in Walker's house in South Parade, while the Patriotic Society (which consisted—according to a later police report—of working men) used his warehouse at the back of the living quarters. And the secretary of the Reformation Society (also mainly working class), John Stacey, writing to Daniel Adams of the London C.I.S., says that "the cause of Liberty goes on rapidly in this Town, our Society meets weekly and we enlist new Members every time. We should have been more numerous had not the influence of the Aristocrats hunted us out of the Public House where we met. . . . We presently rallied our Members and took a private House to meet in . . . and are going to publish a fresh Declaration and we have not the least doubt but when it appears it will be the Means of increasing our Society prodigiously." The letter is to be answered, says Stacey, at the address of William Gorse, New Cross.[1]

The refusal of these people to be boycotted and intimidated was exceedingly irritating to the authorities, locally and nationally. But as yet they hesitated to lay hands on individuals. Their offensive was a general one, launched directly at the mind of the public, aiming at scaring people off the Radical movement, and at forming anti-French and pro-Tory opinion.

At first the government's propaganda efforts were not very effective; they consisted mainly of getting paragraphs favourable to the Ministry printed in the local Press, and distributing two reactionary newspapers, *The Sun* and *The True Briton*. Thomas Walker remarked that "in many public-houses throughout the kingdom you see none but such contemptible papers as *The Sun* and *The True Briton*".[2]

---

[1] Treasury Solicitor's Papers, 3495, p. xxxv.   [2] Walker, *Review*, p. 25.

A useful embryo organisation existed in the Church and King clubs, but an organising genius was needed to exploit their possibilities.

Such a genius eventually appeared, during the autumn of 1792, in the shape of Mr. John Reeves, an ex-justice of Newfoundland, lately returned to England to practise at the Bar. He was moved to profound horror and indignation at the success of the popular societies, and set to work to counteract their malignant influence by a patriotic movement led by eminent and wealthy gentlemen of arch-reactionary ideas.

The first meeting of his organisation, which was called "the Society for Preserving Liberty and Property against Republicans and Levellers", was held at the Crown and Anchor Tavern in the Strand, on 20th November, 1792, when a long "Consideration" was published, with a number of resolutions, the most important being, first, "that the persons present do become a Society for discouraging and suppressing seditious Publications . . . and for supporting a due execution of the laws, made for the protection of persons and property". Secondly, that the society "do use its best endeavours occasionally to explain those topicks of publick discussion which have been so perverted by evil-designing men".

At a later meeting these aims are enlarged upon: "One of the duties . . . is to encourage persons to form similar societies in different parts of the town . . . to check the circulation of seditious publications of all kinds, whether newspapers or pamphlets, or invitations to club-meetings, by discovering and bringing to justice not only the authors and printers of them, but those who keep them in shops, or hawk them in the streets for sale; or what is much worse, are employed in circulating them from house to house. . . . ."

Another self-imposed duty is "by reasoning and by circulating cheap books and papers, to undeceive those poor people who have been misled by the infusion of opinions dangerous to their own welfare and that of the State". The organisers insist on the importance of "acting in subordination to the Magistrate and the Executive Government and in their aid and support". "Wicked men, by the means of Clubs and associations, have been spreading among the simple and ignorant, seditious opinions. . . . Good men associate to counteract those evil designs. . . . To associate in the form which *they* do, is always seditious, and very often treasonable; they all appear to be offenders against the law. To meet as is now proposed, for suppressing sedition . . . and for aiding the magistracy . . . the law allows it, and the time requires it."[1]

At another meeting Mr. Reeves' London Association "earnestly recommends to all good Subjects, whether Masters of Private Families, or Keepers of Inns, Taverns, or Coffee-Houses, to discontinue and discourage the use and circulation of all disloyal and seditious Newspapers".

Thereafter a stream of pamphlets, poems, dissertations poured from the Press: "One Pennyworth of Truth from Thomas Bull to his Brother John"; "The English Freeholder's Catechism"; "An Antidote against French Politics"; "A Parish Clerk's Advice to the Good People on the present Times"; "Dialogue between a Tradesman and his Porter"; "Analysis and Refutation of Paine's *Rights of Man*"; "Questions to the People of Great Britain"; "Think a Little"; and many more.

These were interspersed with broadsheets such as "A Word to the Wise" ("A New Ballad on the Times") which begins:

> The Mounseers, they say, have the world in a string,
> They don't like our Nobles, they don't like our King.
> But they smuggle our wool and they'd fain have our Wheat,
> And leave us poor Englishmen nothing to eat.

It ends:

> Then stand by the Church and the King and the Laws,
> The Old Lion still has his teeth and his claws. . . .

Another, called "The Happy Man", has these lines:

> When my day's work is done, to the alehouse I fly,
> And there I hear all the fine chatter,
> A deal about Freedom and Equality
> And such like nonsensical matter. . . .
>
> I think that they all want to be at the top,
> Who make about Freedom this sputter;
> But if o'er the milk the cream did not pop,
> How could we get any good butter?

[1] Collected Publications of Reeves' Association.

The refrain of this song is "Neighbours, mind this, and be quiet".[1]

There is no indication of the extent of the circulation, or of the effect of all this, but unless the eighteenth-century British workman was very different from his great-great-grandsons of to-day, it seems more than a little doubtful that the appeal would cut much ice with him, or induce him to "be quiet".

John Reeves' activity developed another more important and more sinister side; he was in close contact with the government's police chiefs, and, it seems clear, at least part-directed the later secret operations against the Radicals, using time-honoured methods of spying, informing, eavesdropping, letter-opening, and also inventing new methods. But this was later on. In 1792, the year in question, there were few agents engaged in spying, and those who were, seem to have been directly responsible to the government, having either been picked up by various ministers, or having introduced themselves, as is the case of a gentleman calling himself Mercator, who wrote on 7th October to Lord Grenville "in the absence of the Rt. Hon. Mr. Dundas", about the Corresponding Society.

He tells him that "the Minds of the People are constantly kept in a State of fermentation by the most seditious and treasonable writings. . . . The sacred character of His Majesty is held up to Public Ridicule. . . . Mr. Thelwall, Horne Tooke, his nephew Mr. Vaughan, lend no small assistance towards exciting the people to *rebellion*."

Mercator offers "to acquaint your Lordship with all their secret machinations—the sign of every house at which they meet—their nights of meeting—the names and places of abode of the most violent . . . and with copies of all their correspondence". He says he believes he "can put out a method that will entirely defeat their intentions", and he asks his Lordship to signify his interest, "in the most guarded manner, in the *Daily Advertiser*", when the spy will "immediately wait upon him and expect the strictest secrecy".[2]

Spies did not present themselves quite so readily in the provinces, and the Solicitor-General had to write round to

---

[1] Collected Publications of Reeves' Association.
[2] Treasury Solicitor's Papers, 3495.

local magistrates asking them to co-operate in suppressing sub-versive activities, and provide themselves with agents to keep an eye on book and pamphlet shops, and to buy up any sedi-tious writings they found. The response was not at all bad; within a few days he had enthusiastic promises of co-operation from Perth, from Leicester, from Bolton ("I shall give you every help"), from Stafford ("I will with pleasure undertake the agency") from Sodbury ("Will most readily do all in my power in complyance with your request for the succour of my King and Country"), from Reading, Stroud, Ipswich and other towns.[1]

The magistrates set about their duties in good earnest; one can see from their letters that they really considered it an honour to be asked to help in the purge of the bookshops; it probably did not occur to them that they and their "agents" were doing anything low or ungentlemanly in buying seditious books from printers who often put themselves to a great deal of trouble to serve them, and faced probable ruin by so doing; the case of James Thompson, printer, of Manchester, throws light on the mentality of the Mancunian magistracy—as we shall see in another chapter, appertaining to the following year.

This mentality—stimulated as it was by Home Office approval and Mr. Reeves' example—was to be revealed in its most glaring aspects one night in December, 1792, to Thomas Walker in particular. From then onwards he and his progressive friends realised what to expect from the arm of the law—although their worst expectations were to fall short of the harsh reality.

[1] Treasury Solicitor's Papers, 3495.

## CHAPTER IX

## RIOTS (1792, Winter)

THE events that led up to the disastrous 11th December had best be left to Walker's pen.

"On the 1st of December, 1792," he writes, "His Majesty's Ministers issued their second proclamation, and on the 11th the friends to high church principles in Manchester resolved to follow the example which seems to have been held out at London as a pattern for the whole kingdom by what is called Mr. Reeves' Association.

"The newspapers at Manchester, particularly Harrop's, had long teemed with inflammatory paragraphs against the friends of freedom, or Jacobins, as it then was . . . the fashion to call them."

Walker quotes some passages from the violently anti-jacobin *Mercury*, referring to the radicals as "those levelling societies which would pull down the glorious fabrick of the constitution" and exhorting the loyal to "crush those insidious vipers who would poison the minds of the people, level all distinctions and all property . . .".—"As for those who preach up the equalising principles, . . . they can only be ranked with that class of men whose crimes call loudly for a Gibbet."

And thus, as Walker says, "the minds of the people were incessantly irritated, and the poorer class gradually prepared for the scenes that were to follow".

"In this same week (on 7th December)" he goes on, "a meeting was held in Salford to address his Majesty upon the last proclamation; at this meeting, the same Harrop [proprietor of the *Mercury*, and present Boroughreeve] presided." Among others prominently present were the Reverend John Griffiths, and Richard Unite, deputy constable. The organisers claimed the gathering to be "the most numerous meeting ever remembered on any former occasion, of the inhabitants of this town".

Resolutions were passed professing "the utmost horror and detestation" of jacobinism, and promising "to employ their best efforts to suppress all seditious meetings" and "to co-operate with Government in preservation of peace and good order".

They also announced the formation of an "Association"—"with no other object in view but the PUBLIC GOOD"—and their intention of holding "another meeting for the same purpose at the Bull's Head, Manchester, for the 11th of the same month".[1]

Thomas Cooper voiced a general suspicion that something more than the PUBLIC GOOD was the object behind these meetings: in a leaflet dated 10th December and signed Sydney, he wrote that "by the unregulated interference in Dutch politics, by the proclamation offering bounties to seamen, and by . . . the sudden equipment of ships of the line, WAR appears to be the present determination and the real cause of all the sudden ASSOCIATIONS and loyal declarations".

In an effort to counteract Tory propaganda, Cooper appealed to the inhabitants of Manchester to "pause awhile on behalf of your own interests, and consider what class of ye can be benefited by WAR". He asks, "will landed property become more valuable? . . . Will it [war] diminish the excise, or the land tax, or the house tax, or the window tax, or the commutation tax, or any of the long, long catalogue of taxes which lie so heavy upon this devoted country? . . . The ignorance and bigotry of Church and King politics may deprive us at a stroke of every market for our manufactures which the world affords. . . . Suppose for a moment that the rich and opulent manufacturer can support this—what will the little maker, the country dealer say to such a crisis of affairs? . . ."

And "what will the Weaver say to this? who already finds his wages fallen, his reeds called in, and employment scarce?"

As for the poor, "they are liable to be torn from their families by the violence of the press-gang, while the rich and the luxurious repose in peace upon their beds of down".

Addressing the "loyal" Tory supporters of war, Cooper cries: "Headlong promoters of self-destruction, look round upon the habitations of misery, and pause for a few moments on the consequence of your proceedings, to the wretched possessors of them. . . . You well know . . . that the present politics of every

[1] Walker, *Review*, pp. 45-50.

court in Europe lean to *War with the French*. . . . Ye are apprized
of the HOSTILE PREPARATIONS making in this kingdom, and can
ye be blind to the purpose of them? Again, consider if a war
should happen, what will become of the poor, or whose property will be safe? . . . The consequences are with yourselves,
and the blood upon your own heads. . . ."

He finished by appealing to them, at their meeting "to
address his Majesty, that he would be graciously pleased to
remove from his councils all Ministers hostile to the peace of
the country, and take such measures as are most effectual to
prevent the dangers of impending war".[1]

Walker remarks regretfully that "these forewarnings had
however no effect".—"The meeting which was called for the
11th was held about 12 o'clock of the same day", and no resolutions for a peace policy were put forward. Very much the reverse.

The *Chronicle* reported that "the room was crowded in a
manner never before known" to hear Robert Peel, truest of
Tories and rabid anti-jacobin, make his speech, and "all was
unanimity and the most pleasing loyal attachment".

Soon after the meeting broke up Walker was informed "that
there prevailed a report of a riot that was to take place in the
evening, but looking upon it as an idle report I paid no attention to it". Later he heard that "the people were encouraged
and irritated, by various persons, to raise violent outcries
against the Jacobins and Presbyterians. . . . This went on for
about two hours when the people were, by liquor and other
means, sufficiently inflamed for any mischievous undertaking."

When Walker spoke of "the people" he was not referring to
the hundreds of sober artisans and craftsmen who worked the
new machines, and did skilled work with hand and mind, read
Tom Paine's books, and had the rudiments of political knowledge. The mob that night, like the mob at Birmingham, was
made up of the most unskilled, poorest of the workers, who
from lack of any organisation or education whatsoever were
easy victims to the propaganda of the Church and King club,
and with a little drink and encouragement would act accordingly; there were plenty of hooligan and even criminal elements, about too, who asked nothing better than some excuse

[1] Walker, *Review*, pp. 50-4.

to run wild and riot, and no lack of unscrupulous agents ready to inflame them with fiery language and strong liquor.

That there was planning behind it all was evident to Walker. "Everything now seemed to wear the appearance of a preconcerted scene," he observes. "The same contrivances were used as at a contested election. Parties were collected in different public houses, and from thence paraded the streets with a fiddler before them and carrying a board on which was painted CHURCH AND KING in large letters."

About 7 o'clock in the evening the mob collected before the shop of Falkner and Birch where the *Manchester Herald* was printed. They "attacked the shop and house with stones and brick bats till the windows were almost entirely destroyed and beat in at the front of the building". Many respectable gentlemen "endeavoured to interest those whose duty it was to suppress [these proceedings]" but this apparently "produced nothing but encouragement to the mob".

Poor Matthew Falkner, whose house was under attack, sent a friend, Allen Jackson, to the senior Constable, asking for protection, and was told "Unite [the deputy constable] has orders how to act". Unite had been told "to get together as many persons as he could to oppose any riot should there be one".

Jackson went away deeply dissatisfied, to shouts of "Kick him out of doors", "they have brought matters to this, let them take the consequence", and so on.

It was small wonder that Jackson was not satisfied, in view of what we know of Unite. Eyewitness accounts of the deputy constable's behaviour bear out the picture of an unscrupulous bully with the deepest detestation of everything progressive. One gentleman, "a staunch friend to the King and constitution as any man in Manchester, went to Mr. Harrop's [of the *Mercury*, in the same square] and there found Unite, to whom he said, 'Why don't you go and quell yon mob at Falkner's door? Depend upon it there will be some mischief done, and though I am no friend either to him or his principles, yet I would not have his property hurt.' Unite's answer was 'Oh, let them alone, they are loyal subjects, let them frighten him a bit.' "

Another gentleman, "seeing two men knocking violently at

the door with one hand, and with the other waving their hats
and shouting ... observed Unite go up to them, and tapping
them on the shoulder ... distinctly say 'Good Lads, good Lads!'
then turning round he said, smiling, 'I can keep them quiet by
giving them good words ...' then seeing the beadles standing
near the window, he said to them in a angry tone ...
'Come away from the house! d—n his house, don't come
near it!' "

A third observer says this behaviour was construed by the
mob "as a tacit invitation to the commission of unrestrained
depredations". This observer "followed them several hours and
was astonished to see them go on in their mad career from
hour to hour uninterrupted, when I sincerely believe half a
dozen resolute men were sufficient to have dispersed them".

They were "repeatedly reanimated by persons of respectable
appearance who went among them whenever they seemed to
droop, and applauded and cheered them, sometimes with
whispers, sometimes with 'Church and King for ever, Lads,
down with the Rump', etc., etc."

Yet another witness mentioned that he "saw the Reverend
Mr. Justice Griffith among the mob, a quiet spectator of the
riot"; this witness "ran to fetch Birch that they might apply to
Griffith to read the riot act; on their return they could not find
Griffith". True-blue Tory and chief conspirator in the plot
against the democrats, it was small wonder that Mr. Griffith
did not put himself out to quell the riot.

Our witness went with Samuel Birch to Mr. Bentley, another
magistrate, and got him out of bed; the three of them then proceeded to the houses of several other magistrates, including Mr.
Nathaniel Milne, perhaps the most enthusiastic anti-jacobin of
all, and an ardent co-operator with the Solicitor-General in
the matter of seizing seditious literature. Milne said "it was a
scandalous, shameful, abominable business to call out a
magistrate on such a trifling piece of business as the breaking
of a few windows; that he and a party of constables had just
been at Falkner and Birch's shop and all was very quiet; that
there were only a few windows broken by a few *chance* stones".

When Birch mentioned the inactivity of the constables,
Milne told him to get out of his house. The three men returned

to the shop, where they "found the mob pelting the windows with stones as hard as they could". According to another eye-witness, "some peaceable citizens exclaimed against all this and often endangered their own lives". He himself "chanced to say that such behaviour was very unfair, when one of them said Mr. Falkner's house ought to be pulled down to the ground, and damned them who did not think so too, and told me further that he would knock me down that moment if he knew me to be of the same way of thinking with Mr. Falkner!" One of the special constables was heard to say, in another part of the town, "I'll give you a guinea for every one of the Jacobins' houses you pull down"—though it hardly seems to have been necessary to offer such an incentive at that moment!

Much as they disliked Falkner and Birch, the mob eventually tired of throwing stones at the shop, and turned their attention to Thomas Walker, whom their instigators disliked even more, and could never forgive for his influence or for his support for the popular societies.

A large crowd broke away from Market Square at about 7 o'clock, to surge along to St. Mary's Parade and attack the premises where Jacobin Walker lived and allowed the societies to meet. They swarmed around the door, shouting, and shat-tered some windows, then went away.

"Expecting their return," writes Walker, "and having been informed of the treatment that Mr. Allen Jackson had met with, I determined to defend myself. A gentleman from the country had dined with me; the Constitutional Society, on whose account all this mischief seems to have been prepared, had met at my house that evening, and fortunately for the first time several members of the Patriotic and the Reformation Societies were likewise there. Foreseeing the danger I was exposed to, these gentlemen very kindly agreed to assist me in defending my house and warehouses, in which my brother and I had manufactured goods and unwrought materials to a very large amount."

Walker asked George Wakefield, a member of the Society, to go to the Senior Constable, "and to represent to him what was going forward". Wakefield went, and got the same answer as Jackson, with the added comment: "I wish to God they

THOMAS COOPER

MR.  HARROP

would raze Falkner's house to the ground although it is my own."

When Walker heard this, he realised that "to prevent the scenes of Birmingham being repeated in Manchester, and to save our houses from being burnt and plundered, it was necessary to look for safety to ourselves alone.

"The mob soon returned a second time to my house, broke some windows and retreated. The same happened a third time when I attempted to expostulate with them, but in vain. The clamour was too loud for me to be heard. During these attacks ... none of the town magistrates came to my assistance ... nor the special constables, consisting of near two hundred. We were left to ourselves, just in the same manner as Dr. Priestley ... etc., etc., were at Birmingham. A regiment of dragoons was in the town; they got booted and under arms, both officers and men; and were ready to disperse the rioters, but no measure was taken of that or any other kind.

"About ten o'clock the mob returned to my house the fourth time. Their rancour was now much increased by additional encouragement and liquor (which was given them at several places in the town) and not being molested in their proceedings by persons in authority, it was natural for them to regard it as a tacit approbation of their conduct.

"Fearing lest some of my friends might be too hasty", Walker goes on, "I locked up all the arms I had, giving the key of the room they were placed in to a gentleman on whose coolness I could depend."

The only arms he had, in fact, that could have been of any use, were a few muskets; there were in the house also half a dozen little "swivels"—guns that turn on pivots—which had been adapted for his children to play with, and were perfectly harmless; they had been let off on one or two state occasions, such as the Prince of Wales' birthday, and the night of the repeal of the Fustian Tax; there were also a couple of bayonets and some broadswords, but these were more in the nature of antiques than weapons of war or revolution.

Walker's account continues: "While the mob kept at a distance and contented themselves with destroying my windows, I was under no apprehension from their drunken fury. But at

G

last they shewed a resolution of entering the house, breaking the inner shutters of a room on the ground floor, and attempting repeatedly to force the street door. I tried a second time to pacify them but all was to no purpose; at last a stone struck me on the head; I then fired into the air. Upon this they retreated a little, but afterwards they returned to the attack. Several muskets were then fired over their heads, upon which they all ran away: whether any persons were hurt I have not been able to ascertain; I hope and believe not, as the industry of our enemies would not have failed . . . to have made their names public."

The first of our eye-witnesses described the attack on the house from a vantage point outside, corroborating Walker's report; he adds that "a neighbouring magistrate, Mr. Bentley, came soon after the firing and harangued the rioters upon the impropriety of treating a fellow citizen in such an illegal manner, who, he said, had been so great a friend to the town of Manchester. His voice was soon stifled with 'Down with the Rump', etc., etc."

At last, when everything was perfectly quiet, thanks to Walker's slight display of force, the arm of the law appeared in the shape of Mr. Joseph Hardman, chief senior constable, and several special constables, with Mr. Bentley. They came into the house, and according to Walker, their conversation with him went something like this:

WALKER. Gentlemen, I must confess I find your conduct highly negligent, to say the least—our manufactures, and warehouses were in danger of being destroyed by the unruly mob, and our lives, and those of our families, left to its mercy, just as in Birmingham.

THE GENTLEMEN (*after an awkward silence*). Yes, Mr. Walker, it is regrettable. . . .

WALKER. Regrettable! (*Snorts*).

HARDMAN. Sir, we would appeal to you to fire no more. If the mob should return, Mr. Walker . . .

WALKER. For the fifth time!

BENTLEY. You will certainly be protected by the civil power.

WALKER. As long as that is the case, nothing is farther from my thoughts than to hurt anyone of the multitude. I can't help considering them as being the mere instruments of men with much baser minds and much more sordid views, even if in superior stations of life.

HARDMAN. Then you will not fire any more, sir?

WALKER. If I can count upon your protection, I certainly will not.

With this promise on Walker's part they went away, and Thomas was not molested again that night. But he was not to be left in peace for long. "The next morning (12th December) some hundreds of people assembled in St. Mary's churchyard, before my house. Amongst them was a man haranguing, and reading the contents of a printed paper. What it was I did not hear . . . but I have been told . . . that he urged them strongly to pull down my house or to set it on fire, and that the paper was of a most inflammatory nature.

"Not having any dread of an English mob when they are sober," Walker continues, "I went out to them and expostulated on the proceedings of last night. . . . I was received with the cry of 'Jacobin, damn the Jacobins, damn Tom Paine, down with the Rump', but after a short address to them on the impropriety of their conduct on the preceding evening, and a declaration that I should under the same circumstances defend my house in the same manner again . . . I went away with little exclamation on their part, and no molestation."

That evening "there was some reason to apprehend a repetition of the former outrages". Several friends stayed with Thomas, and during the course of the evening he records that "one of the most respectable characters of the town came to me as from authority, and told me that among the persons in my house were some very obnoxious to the populace; and that while they staid with me it was impossible to answer for the safety of my house and warehouses, but if they were dismissed I might be assured the peace-officers would be able to protect me". One can imagine the expression on Walker's face at receiving this "assurance" on such terms. As might have been expected of him, "the suggestion of turning out of my house one of those friends who, from personal regard to me, and at a personal risque to themselves had come to assist in my protection, I did not comply with".

It would be interesting to know just which of Walker's friends was referred to by the "respectable character" as especially obnoxious to the population. There was no particular reason for the mob to dislike the Constitutional Society's committee—Samuel Jackson or Dr. Collier or Thomas Cooper, who were probably there—any more or any less than William Gorse or George Lomax or John Stacey of the working-class Reformation Society; the truth, much more likely, was that it was the "respectable" persons themselves who objected to the presence of "the lower order of people" in the house and company of a man like Walker, who was one of the upper ten of Manchester. It was carrying democracy rather too far, and offering a (to them) dangerous precedent that Thomas should be allied with and protecting such elements.

Just as Pitt and his friends disliked the "new look" of Reform, because of its combination of middle-class and proletarian supporters, so the respectable characters of Manchester disliked the look of the new alliance between the merchant and mechanics. But Walker knew that those were the people he could really count on, and in fact that they were his only real friends, apart from his very trustworthy servants and his own family. He referred touchingly to the latter in a note to young Watt, shortly after the event (10th February, 1793) saying: "My wife behaves nobly . . . her conduct the morning after the riot I must inform you of: The Constables and about a dozen of their *friends* came to me, offering me the protection of the Civil Power if I would promise not to fire again, and begging me to go off for a few days (alias to run away) the people they said were so exasperated against me. . . . I told them . . . it was in vain to say anything, for that I would never leave my House until I was a corpse; they began to entreat my wife to go, but she immediately stopped them by saying 'While Mr. Walker stays I will stay, so shall my children . . . and if one falls we will all fall together.'"[1] The older children assured their parents they did not mind; and although one of the maids, Martha Wilkinson, was a little nervous (and no wonder), the whole family stayed on at South Parade.

Thomas Walker collected some few extra muskets from his

[1] Walker-Watt Correspondence.

country house at Barlow, in case of further riots, and says that "the fact that the rioters were in much more danger than myself and knew it" accounted for their not attacking the house the following evening—"notwithstanding the multitudes of people who assembled with their usual cries of 'Church and King'. But they went into other quarters of the town, where the same precautions which I had taken were not used; and they destroyed without interruptions the windows and furniture of a house in Great Newton Street"—that of William Gorse, secretary of the Reformation Society, and where that society used to meet.

A week later, Walker wrote to Daniel Adams of the Constitutional Information Society in London, that "all is quiet and I have no doubt will continue quiet if the people are left to themselves; or rather the Mob, as the people, in my opinion, are with us".

"The attack upon Falkner's and Birch's house and shop was, I have no doubt, premeditated, and done with a view to put a stop to the further publication of that paper; so that violence was to accomplish what Law could not; this I conceive to be an outrage of the most atrocious nature."[1]

Violence did not, in fact, accomplish its object; on 22nd December the *Manchester Herald* editorial remarked that "a report is being very industriously circulated that the Herald would no longer be published. We are happy to inform our friends and readers that, in spite of all attempts to check circulation, the sale of it has for many weeks past constantly and very CONSIDERABLY ENCREASED."

And as if to end this gloomy and disturbing chapter on a brighter note, the *Herald* gives a paragraph of tribute to "the numerous body of Irish settled in this town, for their peaceable and exemplary conduct during the late *disgraceful* riots here. We understood that great numbers of them have of late acquired a habit of reading and obtaining knowledge, which is a certain means to peaceful conduct."

[1] Treasury Solicitor's Papers, 3495.

## CHAPTER X

# THE MANCHESTER LOYAL ASSOCIATION
## (1792-1793, Winter)

ONE of the more pernicious and permanent results of the day's work was the consolidation of the forces of reaction, in the shape of The Manchester Association for Preserving Liberty, Order and Property; this was formed at the "Loyal" meeting of 11th December, "to support the Laws, to protect the Inhabitants of this Country from every kind of Violence, and to discourage any attempt to break in upon the good order of society".

Its members' first pronouncement was an "advertisement" published immediately after the riots, declaring the concern they felt "that any persons should have been induced to commit violence against the person or property of some of their townsmen last night". They proclaimed their determination to "support the Boroughreeve and Constables in preventing such attempts *in future*, and invite their fellow townsmen to exert themselves in preventing every meeting of others that is likely to produce riot and disorder". (Needless to say, any and every meeting called by the Radicals might be considered to be in this category!) The statement was signed by the Boroughreeve, James Ackers, and the constables, and "several of the principal inhabitants of the town".

On reading it, Walker commented that it was singular that they "resolved to prevent such attempts in future"—when it was on the very night when the Association was founded that the democrats' houses were "most riotously attacked" and the night following its foundation that Gorse's house was attacked and destroyed.[1]

The Association swung into action immediately after this, with a public declaration intended to forestall any possible blaming of their friends in authority, and also to soft-pedal the

---

[1] Walker, *Review*, pp. 66-8.

riots. They "thanked the gentlemen of this town, and particularly the special constables, who gave their assistance . . . in
preserving the peace of the town; to the inhabitants in general
for their peaceable behaviour; and to those few who had collected from motives of curiosity, for their readiness to disperse
on being applied to for that purpose". Walker muses as to
whether "the persons thus thanked were the mob who would
have pulled my house down, and who *did* destroy Gorse's?"[1]

The loyal gentlemen may not have been consistent, but they
were certainly energetic, and they lost no time in getting busy.
With such worthies as Dr. John Griffith or Mr. Nathan
Crompton (a Tory merchant, and trade rival of Walker's) in
the chair, they met twice weekly at the Bull's Head—the inn-
keeper registering no objection in this case.

Every member had to sign the "Declaration of Secrecy"
before being admitted into the Committee Room. Minutes
were carefully kept, with notes of those in attendance. There
was supposed to be a magistrate present at every meeting, and
this representative of the law was expected to be of impeccable
loyalty; one of the Committee's orders was "that no attorney
of this Committee be concerned either directly or indirectly
with the defence of, or advice concerning" any person accused
of treason or sedition.

Nor were they in any way passive in regard to such "persons".
They had a sub-committee (known as the "Committee of
Papers") actively engaged in watching for subversive literature,
chiefly through paid agents (the minutes for 14th December,
1792, record an order "that a reward of 10 Guineas . . . be given
to any person who will . . . give such evidence as will discover
and bring to justice any person guilty of writing, printing, publishing, or dispersing seditious and treasonable writings, books
and papers".) Other activities were "considering" their finds,
and disposing of them to the authorities in London ("that the
*Manchester Herald* of 22nd December be recommended to the
consideration of the Committee of Papers . . . Messrs Milne and
Sergeant be requested to send Falkner's last paper to the
solicitors of the Treasury and to desire they will give such
opinion as they may think fit"); they decided on action against

[1] Walker, *Review*, p. 68.

the popular societies ("that the Members of the Constitutional Society be called upon to declare their names"); they ordered large quantities of literature from the London Association (Reeves')—"2,000 of leaflets at 6/- a 100" is a typical order, and one which shows that their financial position left nothing to be desired; they sent messages of support to other local Associations, of which Manchester and district boasted several: including one at Ardwick, which met at the Rose and Crown, and another at Salford, in the Black Swan; messages of welcome were directed to the "Catholic Inhabitants" for their declaration of loyalty on 22nd December.[1]

Walker did not know the full extent of all this activity, but he realised that his enemies were powerful and busy, and he decided he must get public opinion on his side before they did. He published an "Address to the Inhabitants of Manchester" to clear himself of any calumnious rumours about the firing on the crowd, and to prove his good intentions.

He pointed out that "no charge of riot or tumult . . . had ever been made against the Friends of the People", and he asked: "Why then have I been insulted?—whom have I injured, or what Offence have I committed? If it be a crime to enlighten the People respecting their just rights, I have been guilty of this crime, and to the end of my days I shall live in the commission of it."

"Is it a crime," he asks, "to wish the more indigent members of society eased from some of the numerous taxes which they pay in the purchase of every necessary of life? to wish them better lodged, and better fed, and *better instructed*? I am guilty of these crimes. Is it a crime to wish the British Constitution restored to its original purity, and the whole system of Representation freed from Perjury and Corruption?—Of this too I am guilty. Of every good wish to mankind and my country— I am guilty. If the laws of the land have been violated by my conduct, let me be punished according to law; but let not the character of the British Nation be stained by the base and illiberal persecution of one of its most sincere well-wishers.

THOMAS WALKER, 13th December."[2]

[1] Manchester Loyal Association, *Minute Book*.    [2] Walker, *Review*, pp. 67-70.

Of the copious correspondence which followed, there is far too much to quote more than a fraction. The Sheffield Society wrote "to express their sentiments of condolence. . . . It is not only for their patriotic brother and friend that they feel the sensations of sorrow and regret: they feel also for their country, their liberties—and they feel for their dark and deluded countrymen, whom they believe to be the tools of an arbitrary faction."

Thomas replied thanking them, and saying that he also "looked upon the misguided multitude . . . as wretched tools of a most unprincipled faction". This letter, which was published in the newspapers, drew forth an irate retort (also in the Press) from the Boroughreeve and constables, proclaiming their solicitude "for the discovery and punishment of all instigators of riot . . ." and demanding explanations of Walker's accusations: particularly "of whom this wretched and unprincipled faction consists?"

Walker replied that he was glad to learn of their solicitude, for "I am satisfied that no gentlemen can have better means of information . . . it would indeed have been as well if this solicitude had appeared in an earlier stage".

"It remains with you," he writes, "to state to the public how it has happened that . . . [you] have not taken one single rioter into custody?"—"It will not be easy, gentleman," he adds, "to compensate for your supineness, where it was your duty to be active, by your officiousness, where it is your duty to be quiet. . . ." He reaffirms his principles and declares that "no hazard of my person nor of my property shall ever deter me from supporting to the utmost of my abilities, the RIGHTS of the people".

The Boroughreeve and constables returned to the charge with a letter in the *Mercury*, accusing Mr. Walker of "firing on the people with SLUGS" (which is quite untrue if we are to believe Walker's own account), and of "exulting in the use of paltry Subterfuges . . . to elude the most plain and proper Questions". They signed with a flourish, "in the fullest confidence that Truth will prevail".

The Loyal Association followed this up with an effusive vote of thanks to them "for your zeal and attention to the public welfare, your constant exertions for the preservation of peace and tranquillity, but more especially for defending the inhabitants of this town from the false calumnies and malignant imputations against them, and the method you have pursued against the restless and evil-disposed author thereof".

Another resolution congratulated them on their "just and spirited answers to Mr. Thomas Walker's false, infamous and ridiculous Charge".[1]

However bitter these hostile local attacks on him, Walker could take some comfort from the fact that he had support among thousands of sympathisers and champions in the Whig leaders, who brought the matter of the Manchester riots up in the House of Commons several times.

Fox spoke on three different occasions (13th, 15th and 17th December) on the Associations and the dangers of suppression and of provocation. On 13th December he warned the House that "the Declarations of the Associations went to instigate father against son, or neighbour against neighbour. A man comes to another, and says, 'You don't love the Constitution'. —'No! I declare I do, I cherish its principles, and would improve its practice'.—'Aye, aye, now we know you; you would improve, would you? That's only a specious name for seditious purposes'."

On the 15th, Fox declared that "whenever the time shall come when a man shall not dare say he prefers a republican form of government, or a despotic form of government, if either of these notions—equally opposite to our constitution—are his and he dare not utter them, from that time, I date the extinction of that constitution". He asked if it was to be maintained that no discussions concerning government should take place in this country? "After so many of our blessings had resulted from gradual improvement, was it to be said, 'Now we have had enough of improvement, Now we stop!'?"

The Associations, said Fox, though many of them were composed of respectable members, disdained to argue; "but if any man thinks differently from them he is held up as a traitor. Wretched times, when even the name of liberty becomes unpopular!"[2]

[1] Walker, *Review*, pp. 70-86.     [2] *Collected Speeches of Charles James Fox.*

Two days later the Whig leader and Grey both drew the attention of the House to the Associations' share of the responsibility for the recent riots, and Grey specifically attacked Robert Peel for his speech on 7th December at Salford. This greatly disgusted the gentlemen of the Manchester Association, who voted on 21st December "that something be prepared by the Committee of Papers to counteract any bad effects which may arise from Mr. Grey's misrepresentation . . ." and thanked Peel "for the very handsome manner in which he defended the Manchester Association against the unfounded attacks of Mr. Grey".[1]

According to the *Manchester Herald*, Grey had referred to a report of Peel's speech at the Church and King meeting; he had also quoted "a very gross and, in his opinion, libellous reflection on the Dissenters" circulated by the Association, and and had moved "that His Majesty would be graciously pleased to give orders to the Attorney-General to prosecute the authors of the said paper".

Peel defended himself by protesting that "everything in the paragraph (about him) was false—except that he had said 'God save the King' ". He said, referring to the political atmosphere in Manchester, that "Mr. Paine's writings had made very short progress", owing to the good sense of people there, who "would not exchange two shillings for eight pence, or roast beef and plumb-pudding for frogs; nor divide a pair of breeches . . .".

He added, to the indignation of one Hon. Member (Tory) for a Scottish Borough, that "their reading was not as extensive as their brothers in Scotland".

Fox also came back that day to the subject of the Associations "who made such professions of loyalty". He asserted that it was contrary to law for persons to unite for the purpose of carrying on prosecutions. "It was a conspiracy when above a certain number of people supported with money any prosecution, and this opinion he had received many years before from the late Lord Ashburton." There were, he said, two hundred informations given by the Associations on the file for prosecution.

Fox laid the blame for the recent riots squarely on these organisations. "The works of Mr. Paine produced no riots," he

[1] Manchester Loyal Association, *Minute Book*.

pointed out, "but the words Church and King were the pretence
for those disgraceful scenes at Birmingham and . . . at Manchester."

He was shocked at the inflammatory literature put out by
the Associations, which would obviously stir up the worst
emotions among ordinary people and be an almost direct
incitement to violence; and he quoted a pamphlet issued by the
London Association—"A Penny worth of Truth from Thomas
Bull to his Brother John"—which is a most remarkable blend
of anti-jacobinism and anti-semitism. It contains the assertion
"that all Kings are bad cannot be true, because God himself is
one of them. He calls himself King of Kings; which not only
shows us he is a King, but that he has other kings under him.
The Scripture calls Kings *the Lord's Anointed*, but who ever
heard of an anointed Republic?"

Further on it observes "that God never made a King is a
great Lye; did not our Saviour say he was *King of the Jews*? . . .
The Jews who crucified him have never had a King from that
day to this: not because they dislike a King, but because they
are not good enough to have one." If England had no King "we
should be just where the Jews are . . . a monument of the
Divine Wrath, and a disgrace to the world".

We learn, farther on, that the Dissenters and their supporters are like the Devil "who delights to be the author of Misery.
. . . So they massacre poor priests, rob and plunder the country
and their Church, put Kings and Queens in prison, and then
sing Ça ira, for joy that *Hell is broke loose*."[1]

Fox commented in Parliament that "the Association's paper
was likely to produce much more mischief than might be at
first imagined". It preached up the divine right of Kings, "a
doctrine of a more dangerous tendency than any other".

He claimed that "the Dissenters' situation demanded immediate protection. The Manchester outrage against them was a
disgrace to the country." As to Walker (who was not a Dissenter), the merchant "whatever his political principles might be,
was a gentleman of the most excellent character in private life
. . . as such he should be esteemed and respected".

Replying, Windham, the Home Secretary, claimed that as

[1] Collected Publications of Reeves' Association.

the House "had directed no prosecutions on either side, it could not be charged with partiality. The law was equally open in all cases. The indignation excited against Mr. Walker was much more fairly imputable to his political opinions than to his being a Dissenter." Windham thought it natural, even justifiable, for men to feel indignation "against those who promulgated doctrines threatening all that was valuable and dear in society". If there were not means of redress by law, Mr. Windham thought that even violence would be justifiable. "But we had laws, therefore violence ought to be punished"; and he defended the Associations "as tending to prevent violence by giving vigour to the law".[1]

Walker protested strongly against the Home Secretary's defence of the Associations: "Mr. Windham should have recollected that the cry of the rioters and the cry of the Associators is one and the same: 'Church and King,' and 'Down with the Jacobins' is equally in vogue among these worthy coadjutors. Exhilarated by the music of these vociferations, Mr. Windham's respectable Clients proceed to attack the persons and destroy the property of peaceable citizens, and thus do they tend to prevent violence and give vigour to Law!"

As to the suggestion that the House was impartial, this would hardly hold water. The facts and complaints were all on one side, Walker pointed out, so how could the House direct prosecution on both? And since prosecutions had been directed against the rioters at Birmingham, why not against those at Manchester?

Walker poured scorn on Windham's remark: "The Law was equally open to all cases". "The Law, as has been frequently said," commented Walker, "is alike open to the poor and to the rich; and so (said Mr. Horne Tooke on some occasion) is the London Tavern; but they will give you a very sorry welcome, unless you come with money sufficient to pay for your entertainment." As to the promulgation of doctrines: "Mr. Windham did not state, because Mr. Windham could not state, what doctrines I have ever promulgated of this description. . . . I have never propagated any doctrines but the doctrines of peace and good will towards men: I have never

[1] Debrett's *Parliamentary Register*, XXXIV, p.165.

ventured like Mr. Windham . . . to justify acts of violence
against my neighbour—because he differed from me in
*political opinion.*"

He added that even savages "never punish mere differences
of opinion; they confine their revenges to real, not to fancied
injuries".[1]

One thing emerges, when the dust settles after the welter of
polemic and counter-polemic, congratulations, curses, condo-
lences and aspersions: the popular societies were undaunted, and
ready to fight on. The Constitutional, Patriotic and Reformation Societies raised their voices in unison again on 20th
December, with a congratulatory message to Fox, and a declaration of their determination to go on working for a parliamentary reform. "When no doubt can reasonably remain,"
they say, "but that the voice of the House of Commons shall be
the voice of the nation—then, and not till then, will the
Manchester societies be satisfied . . . and relax their efforts in
this public cause."

They also "exhort their fellow citizens to meet peaceably but
firmly on every convenient opportunity, for the purpose of
investigating . . . the Constitution under which they live; that
public ignorance and ancient prejudice may no longer stand in
the way of salutary reformation . . .". The address ends with a
plea for peace between England and France, by the societies,
who "scruple not to avow their anxiety, that this country may
not be induced by any courtly machinations whatever, to join
the band of continental despots, now leagued against the
liberties of mankind".[2]

This courageous statement is in striking contrast to one
published shortly after—in the *Manchester Herald* of 29th December—by a large number of Dissenters of Manchester and Salford, dissociating themselves completely with their defenders,
and declaring "that we are steadily and affectionately attached
to the British Constitution and convinced of the Excellence of
the Principles on which it is erected".

One might have expected some expression of solidarity with
those who had been persecuted, but this is sadly lacking.

The politically minded Radicals in Manchester were left

[1] Walker, *Review*, pp. 87-92.          [2] Ibid., pp. 92-6.

to carry on their struggle for reform single-handed. At the very time when the battle was sharpening—when the Tories were consolidating their ranks, and when unity between all those who needed reform and peace was most to be desired, and could have achieved good results—the middle-class Whigs and Dissenters dropped off through caution, apathy, dislike of association with the workers who were becoming more and more interested in the Rights of Man, whatever Robert Peel might say. These "moderates" were more afraid of being labelled Jacobin than of being dragged into war. The working-class reformists determined to carry on without them. And although Walker tells us that the Declaration of 20th December was "their last recorded statement", the Reformation Society, its weavers and labourers undaunted, published at least one more declaration—in the *Mercury* of 23rd March, 1793—of their determination "to evince to the World that we are the friends of *Peace and Good Order* and not the contrary". They suggested that the Associations "ask whether Anarchy and Confusion have not dwelt in *their* character"; and finally invite "every well wisher to the Liberty and Happiness of his Country to join us in our efforts to regain universal suffrage and annual elections—without which we cannot be called Freeman nor Britons".

## CHAPTER XI

# WAR FEVER AND WITCH-HUNT
### (1793, Spring)

WAR, in spite of all the efforts and protests of the Radicals, broke out early in 1793. The French declared it, on 1st February, and blame for the outbreak of hostilities was laid by the British Government and its supporters on the Republic.

In fact, the declaration of war was the inevitable climax of the tension which had been mounting between the two countries for several months. The chief causes were, on the one hand, the open support given by the British to the emigré monarchists, and to Austrian and Prussian aggression, not to mention the suppression of sympathy for the Jacobins in England, and the obvious desire to destroy the Paris government and its achievements.

On the other hand, the French were asking for trouble when, in a decree of November, 1792, they promised help to their supporters abroad in internal struggles against reactionary governments; and when they violated the Franco-British Commercial treaty of 1786 by sailing down the Scheldt, thus threatening (as Pitt thought) the neutrality of the Netherlands and upsetting the balance of power in Europe. This, and the execution of Louis XVI on 21st January—which roused strong anti-French feelings among many good-natured English people, and must have been thought likely to sway the country's opinion in favour of a war—were the main factors which determined Pitt to abandon neutrality; for although the actual declaration of war was made by France, the British Government had already caused a rupture (under the terms of the 1786 treaty) when it dismissed the French Ambassador, M. Chauvelin, immediately after the death of the King.

There seems no reason to doubt that Pitt's ministry expected, and possibly did not object to, war with France sooner or later; it would certainly appear so, from King George's message of

JAMES WATT, JUNIOR

MRS. HANNAH WALKER
*by Wright of Derby*

28th January, announcing the ambassador's dismissal and the
further augmentation of the British armed forces, and proclaiming his "intention to take the most effective measures for
maintaining the Security and Right of his own Dominions, for
supporting his Allies, and for opposing views of aggrandisement
and ambition on the part of France".

There must have been many of his subjects who wondered
whether France was really contemplating aggrandisement at
our expense, and whether we had any right, or reason, to break
off relations on account of a purely internal question—however
much one disapproved of regicide.

In spite of the natural revulsion against the executions, and
of the anti-republican feeling fostered by the government, the
opinion of many people was expressed in some verses published
as a broadsheet at the end of January:

> England! the death of Louis calls aloud
> REFORM! and PEACE proclaim with all MANKIND.
> Revenge belongs to God! Shall British Blood
> Be spilt for nought? Forbid it every Mind![1]

Not great poetry, perhaps, but significant of a general feeling
among those who realised what war would mean.

Lord Stanhope put these misgivings plainly enough, in the
House of Lords on 2nd February: "In the Franco-British
Treaty . . . it was expressly decreed that in case of misunder-
standing arising between the nations, the sending away the
Ambassador of one of them should be deemed a rupture. . . .
M. Chauvelin had been ordered away in a most ignominious
manner."

The noble lord declared roundly that the French declaration
of war upon the British was provoked by hostile acts of Pitt's
government. He was particularly scathing about the inadequate
protection given to our ships: "It has struck the commercial
part of the Public with Astonishment that they have for four
months been goading and provoking the French into war, by
every species of insult, and have taken no adequate precautions
to guard our trade against capture. Ever since 10th August they
have refused to treat with the French Ministry, though they

---

[1] Treasury Solicitor's Papers, 3495.

H

have suffered the most indecent invectives to be thrown against them in journals, the property of their clerks; and though they called on Parliament to sanction an armament and called for pecuniary support for that purpose, our ships were unprotected and unprepared when it came to the point. . . ."

The war may have been inevitable; but the feeling among the people of England, from the Whig peers to the Lancashire weaver was that it was being rushed into and that the government were not doing what they should to avoid it.

The Marquis of Lansdown reminded the House of Commons as early as 26th December, 1792, that "during the American War we negotiated with people whom we called Rebels—why not negotiate with the French?" He also remarked on "the new Associations and on the industry with which alarms were attempted to be raised, but he could easily see that war was the object of the whole".

Thomas Erskine, the future Lord Chancellor, in a passionate and splendid plea for peace, hit out on 17th December at the war profiteers—"the men who, without virtue, labour or hasard are growing rich as their country is impoverished"; who "rejoice when obstinacy or ambition add another year to slaughter and devastation, and laugh at their desks at bravery and Science when they are adding figure to figure, and cypher to cypher, hoping for a new contract as an estate from a new armament, and computing the profits of a siege or a tempest. . . . I will not consent to the ruin of my country by war to oblige such characters.

"I say you should deliberate again and again, before you go to war. . . ."

Whilst Erskine and Stanhope were appealing to members of Parliament in London, the leading provincial Radicals were appealing to the people of their home towns, to bring pressure on the government to pursue a peace policy.

In Manchester, as the threat of war increased, the Constitutional Society decided to reprint Thomas Cooper's "Appeal to the Inhabitants" and to circulate it as widely as possible. The Society for Constitutional Information in London, also, voted that it be "printed in the public papers, and that one hundred thousand copies of the same be printed by this Society and distributed to their correspondents in Great Britain and Ireland".

On 21st December, 1792, however, "the secretary, Daniel Adams, reported to the London society that he had offered the address . . . to the *Morning Chronicle* and *Morning Post*, in order to be published, but that they had refused from the seditious tendency".

The reply of the *Morning Post* was read to the committee: "This excellent paper, drawn by a masterly hand," it said, "we wish to see in the possession of every Englishman, but after the verdict against Mr. Paine . . . the proprietors of newspapers tremble at inserting anything except fulsome panegyrics on a depraved Legislature and hungry Court Minions. The vile associations have worked the public mind into such a fervour that a jury would, by the intimation of a judge, find anything a libel—we therefore can only express our sorrow that self-preservation will not permit us to make the *Morning Post* the vehicle to convey this paper to the public."

Baulked of this channel, the Constitutional Society decided to find another "mode of communication with the public", and appointed a sub-committee to consider the question. It was resolved, in the meantime, "that it be printed in the News-papers in Scotland".[1]

We do not know if the address reached the Scottish public, but it certainly reached the files of the Treasury Solicitor—through the good offices of the Reverend John Griffith of Manchester. According to a pencil note on the margin of the leaflet, Griffith received it "from Mr. Birch, partner to Mr. Falkner".

In picking up and passing on anti-war (and therefore "seditious") literature, with an ulterior motive, Mr. Griffith was only doing the same as his "loyal" colleagues all over the country. There was feverish activity in every town which boasted a magistrate and a bookshop, in response to the request in early December of Mr. White, the Treasury Solicitor. Suspects were being rapidly rounded up. The declaration of war gave an extra fillip to the "loyal" activities, as it was now possible to accuse the Radicals of being traitors to their

[1] Treasury Solicitor's Papers, 3505.

country, in propagating any sentiments of a nature friendly to the French.

From Leicester, Mr. Heyrick, magistrate, wrote apologising to Mr. White for not having replied before: "We have been so busy preparing and preferring indictments of Delinquents here that we could not answer sooner . . ."—but he assured the Treasury Solicitor that he was carrying out the minute instructions which had been given as to the books and pamphlets regarded as suspect: any of the works of Thomas Paine, and *The Jockey Club*. Mr. White had laid down that: "Great care must be taken that the person so obtaining such book or pamphlet do mark them in such a manner before he parts with the same . . . that he may be ever after able to swear to the Identity of the Book or Pamphlet and when, where, and of whom he purchased the same. . . ." If it should transpire that "any other books of a same tendency" were being sold, the magistrate must "transmit them to us in order that you may receive directions whether or not they are judged to be fit objects for prosecution".

Mr. Heyrick was certainly doing his best in Leicester: "I have employed James Jackson to purchase the following Books," he writes, giving a list. "He bought them at the shop of Richard Phillips . . . they were delivered to him by a young man in the shop . . . who is journeyman to Phillips . . . Jackson has marked them all, and lodged them with me. He will be able to identify them, and to prove completely when and of whom he had them. . . . In the meantime you may rely on every Exertion which the most anxious Interest in the subject can afford." He adds that Phillips "is the Printer of a violently Republican Newspaper here, called the Herald, and is at the head of a Society of Painites".

Napean, one of the London Solicitors of the Treasury, comments to White, that "Phillips is a very seditious fellow, and it will be extremely desirable that his conduct should be marked, but I fear from what Mr. Heyrick states that the Pamphlets . . . were obtained from the shopman and not from Phillips himself". Heyrick was trying to make sure that the culprit did not slip through his fingers: "I have observed your Directions about taking and watching Phillips's newspapers," he writes, "and have used the same caution with respect to another which is published by a Mr. Combe, and generally contains doctrines more levelling even than those of the former." He adds that "both have become much more moderate lately. I don't mean to impute this to a change of Principles but to Fear."

In Ipswich, Charles Squire, a magistrate, "made some little inquiry and found that the Rights of Man and some few other works of that order have been sold in this town"; he is however not worried: "the hint I gave the booksellers will, I believe, prevent their sale in future". He mentioned incidentally that "a Disputing Club had been instituted at one Alehouse here, consisting of very Inferior People, and it was last week dispersed by the Magistrates of the Town".

From Stafford, Mr. John Collin was happy to say "the Magistrates were being particularly active in suppressing all sorts of seditious writing and in taking notice of a person who speaks unfriendly towards government. . . " and he enclosed a notice of a county meeting of "the Noblemen, Gentlemen, Clergy, Freeholders, and other Inhabitants of the County". Yet in nearby Newcastle-under-Lyme Thomas Fenton regretted that "Paine's publications are in the hands of most of the people in this neighbourhood, and particularly of the Journeymen Potters".

As time went on, more and more printers and publishers appeared in court, and escaped or got severe punishments according to the juries' political tendencies. Mr. Heyrick had "no hesitation in saying that a Borough Jury (in Leicester) may be trusted—both the Grand and Petit Juries will be formed of the most respectable of the Tradesmen, and there is *but one opinion among them here*". In Warrington, according to Mr. William Maine, the jury was equally trustworthy: "Hooton was tried on Wednesday afternoon and found guilty. The Judge sentenced him to two years' imprisonment, and to be once sat in the Pillory with a Board over his Head, stating him to be a seditious and ungrateful subject. . . ."

On the other hand, Mr. Goodwin of Derby writes on 10th April of one Bower, had up for Libel at the Quarter Sessions: "Although every necessary proof was made, the Jury, after being locked up three hours, brought him in Not Guilty: because they say it did not appear it was done with a view to raise commotion or disturbance in the County." One can almost hear his sigh of despair as he adds: "If I wished to publish a most violent libel, I would do it in the County of Derby!"

The same could not be said of the county of Lancashire. In Manchester the investigators were especially active, thanks to the untiring and virulent energy of the Rev. John Griffith and his father, not to mention Messrs. Harrop, Crompton, Unite and company, on the one hand, and the financial backing and organisation of the well-connected Association on the other.

In the matter of collecting seditious literature no stone was left unturned, and no means despised; one example of the methods used by those chiefly responsible, Messrs. Milne and Sergeant the magistrates, is worth quoting. They sent a young man called Hallows to buy a copy of *The Jockey Club* at James Thompson's shop in Market Street. According to Hallows' account, Thompson—an honest democrat with a good reputation as a citizen and as a bookseller—received him courteously, but "said *The Jockey Club* had been much called for, that he had sold numbers of them, and therefore had not one in the shop, but should have them done on Thursday". Hallows replied that "he could not wait till that time, as he wanted it to send to a friend in the county". Thompson then remembered that his friend, Jonathan Slack, further down Market Street, had a copy; he suggested Hallows "go to him with Thompson's compliments, and request him to let him have *The Jockey Club* which Thompson had bound up for him and tell him he (Slack) should have another on Thursday . . .".[1]

It was perhaps only natural that Milne, yearning to ingratiate himself with the Treasury Solicitor and persons in the Ministry, should take advantage of the decency and unguarded goodwill of the democrats; by this little piece of deception the magistrate got his *Jockey Club*, and the law got its man—for James Thompson was, sure enough, had up and committed for trial on 18th April of that year, with the usual result of a long term in gaol.

[1] Treasury Solicitor's Papers, 11, 3498.

But individual victims were of no particular interest to the anti-Jacobins, whose aim was the total destruction of the democratic societies and the collective ruin of their members; the Association's committee sedulously collected the names of all suspected democrats in the district, and producted its list—beginning with the names of Walker and Cooper—on 17th January, with a minute to the effect that "the Magistrates be requested to summon the following persons to appear before them as soon as possible to take the oath of allegiance to His Majesty King George III".

As mentioned earlier, the Association's "Committee of Papers" had sent a copy of the *Manchester Herald* to the Treasury Solicitor for his advice on, and approval of, its suppression. Walker got to hear of this, and he told James Watt junior, on 23rd January: "So much enraged that I cannot write. Matthew Falkner and his partner Birch have *each* been served three ex efficio informations from the Attorney General, and to-morrow it is said three or four indictments are to be served against them at the Quarter Sessions and one or two against me, Cooper, Jackson (and others) which I do not believe, however I am determined to see what the Aristocrats will do. . . ."[1]

It was the beginning of the end for the valiant *Herald*; it fought on manfully for a few more weeks, but there was no issue after that of 23rd March. There was no announcement of its closing down, nor any public comment, except for a strange handbill which some enemy produced for the occasion. This was in the form of an obituary notice, surrounded by a black band, and headed: "VIOLENT DISSOLUTION—being the Exit of Mons. Herald of Manchester and near Relation of Mons. Argus of London, who expired on Saturday last to the great regret of the Jacobins, Painites, etc., etc."

The leaflet says "it is imagined that his death was occasioned by an assault of an enormous battery committed upon his body about three months ago" (a reference to the December riots when Falkner's shop was attacked), "but it is well known that he was perfectly recovered". Death was due to "six mortal wounds"—that is, six indictments.

[1] Walker-Watt Correspondence.

"Notwithstanding the boasted number of his friends," the bill goes on, "there were very few attended to pay their last tribute . . . amongst the few artificers (there) a Cooper, a Collier and two famous Walkers were selected to bear the pall."

After an obscure reference to "a huge black Gib Cat" of "great fidelity", meaning Samuel Jackson who was known locally as the Black Cat—the paper reports: "Mons. Herald was interred under the pulpit of his own Kirk, that, as he expressed himself, his very carcass might rekindle in the Orator, the dying spark of Liberty, Equality and the Rights of Man."

The dying spark of Liberty was in fact being bravely guarded by the "jacobins" who refused to be daunted by the loss of their newspaper, by arrests, or by threats of prison and pillory. One example was James Thompson, locked in jail, while one of his handbills (sent by Milne to White in London) was being circulated by his friends; this was headed: "JOHNNY BULL'S REASONS for liking Peace better than War"; and at the bottom was the slogan: "Peace with France, Safe Commerce with the World, and LIBERTY AND OLD ENGLAND FOR EVER! HUZZA!"[1]

Such anti-war leaflets were avidly read and passed round; as the country became more deeply involved and the effects of Pitt's policy began to be seen, the fighters for peace renewed both their efforts to show the futility of bloodshed, and their demands for negotiations with the French. As Thompson's leaflet had it: "What may we lose by a war? and what may we gain?—ALL LOSS and NO GAIN. Nothing but Loss, but Infamy, and Poverty and Taxation and Ruination." The arguments given (too long for quotation here) were borne out by events not much later; even a few months of war showed disastrous effects.

A letter from a Radical minister of the church, Rev. James Fyshe Palmer of Dundee, describes the situation in Scotland in July of that year, and how "the distress occasioned by this mad and unprincipled war is thickening apace in this country".

At Dundee he says, wages have fallen a half. At Glasgow thousands are little short of starvation. "Weavers that could earn thirty shillings a week offer themselves to farmers for only their victuals. A master of a Dundee vessel just arrived says that

[1] Manchester Reference Library Leaflets.

when he was there two people fell dead in the streets of Glasgow, famished for want of food." Bankruptcy and unemployment overshadowed the country: "The manufacturers cannot pay wages in money, they offer goods in payment . . . a weaver brought his webb to one and begged half a crown—it could not be had, he then asked for a shilling, declaring that he had not tasted food for two days."[1]

From Southern England, another writer, the philosopher William Frend (later to be ejected from Cambridge University for his outspoken writing) reported the effect of rising prices and exorbitant taxes:

"Three days after the debate on the King's messages . . . the exclamation of a group of poor women going to market made an impression on my mind which not all the eloquence of the Houses of Lords and Commons can efface. 'We are to be sconced three pence in the shilling . . . we are to be sconced a fourth part of our labour—what is all this for?' I did not dare to tell them. . . ." For, Frend asks, "what is the beheading of a monarch to them? What is the navigation of the Scheldt to them?—Let others talk of glory, let others celebrate the heroes . . . who are to deluge the world with blood; the words of the poor market women will still sound in my ears, we are sconced three pence in the shilling, a quarter of our labour!—for What?"[2]

The price for stamping out freedom abroad and at home was being paid, as always, by the people.

Those who had least to gain, the poor and the humble, paid the most—often with their lives, their health and the life and health of their children. But the middle classes were paying too, with their businesses collapsing, their shops closing, their hopes for a bright future for their families going, if not gone. It was a high price indeed. And it was going to rise higher still.

[1] Treasury Solicitor's Papers 11, 3497.        [2] Ibid.

## CHAPTER XII

## KING'S EVIDENCE (1793, Summer)

THE distribution of anti-war leaflets went on, despite the Association's efforts to prevent it, right into the summer of 1793. It was on 5th June that the first arrest for this "crime" took place.

Benjamin Booth, the miscreant, was an earnest and decent young man who had belonged to the Reformation Society for several months. He made copious notes at the time of his arrest and imprisonment, which he later sent to Thomas Walker, and which threw much light on the conspiracy against the Radicals.

He began by describing how Unite arrested him "for a paper intitled WAR"—Cooper's leaflet, of course—and how he was taken to the Rev. Mr. Griffith, who was very obviously drunk.

Griffith said he was sorry to see Booth: "I had got among a very bad set; and it would be much better if I would give them up". He wanted to know the identity of the author and printer of the leaflet, but Booth refused to say. He tried cajoling and flattery: "said he was surprised I [Booth] should wish to excite discontent in the public mind; my brother was as loyal and as well respected as any man in the town; and before this time I bore an excellent character; all the time speaking in an encouraging stile for me to come into his measures, but finding I was not at all inclined to do so, he . . . said he should demand respectable bail for £50 each".

Booth sent to his brother, who was out, but George McCallum, a member of the Patriotic Society, offered bail—at which Mr. Griffith raised it to £150 each, and said, "Now let Mr. Walker and Mr. Cooper bail you: you know them, I suppose?" To which Booth replied that he did, but cared for them no more than for any other gentlemen of his acquaintance.

Unite then took Booth through the main streets to the New Bailey prison. "He kept discoursing to the crowd," says Booth, "that it was such people as me who had occasioned the war, and he would expose me, wishing at the same time we were all hanged. . . . Now and then the rabble shouted."

Booth was kept all night at the New Bailey, and at 6.30 the next evening Unite took him to Griffith's again. Here he was "left in the lobby", and the parlour door was opened and a number of worthies had a look at him. One of them, Mr. Hulme, said "he was sorry to see him here, as they had been school-fellows", and Booth "was of a respectable family, all of whom he knew very well". He begged Benjamin "not to stand in his own light; begged I would not hurt myself for Mr. Walker, whom he cursed, and said I was worth fifty Mr. Walkers; Mr. Walker had been the destruction of Mr. Matthew Falkner, Mr. Birch, and would be of many others. I replied I thought Mr. Walker a very worthy and respectable gentleman."

A good deal of discussion on whether Booth should be allowed bail then followed, Paynter, an attorney friend of Griffith, saying "any persons who entertained the same prin-ciples [as Booth] should not be allowed to be bail for him".

The poor lad was taken away again by Unite, the gentlemen remarking as he went "that the crowd which was gathered would pull him to pieces", and telling Unite to "expose him to the fury of the populace". Through the main streets they went again—along Hanging-Ditch, through the Market Place, into St. Ann's Square, up Deansgate, down Dolefield—"Mr. Unite discoursing in the same manner as before and the boys shouting".

He was locked up in a cell in the New Bailey, and kept there from 7th to 12th June. He was in solitary confinement, "locked up two hours longer than the rest, and put to bed two hours before the rest", and not allowed to speak privately with his attorney.

On the 12th he was liberated by the bail of two friends for £150 each, and himself for £300.[1] He was completely in the dark as to whether he had been arrested on account of the leaflet, or of his activities in the Reformation Society, or for some other reason. He was to learn soon enough of the far more sinister cause of his first and his later detentions.

Another arrest for distribution of the same anti-war leaflet

[1] Walker, *Review*, pp. 97-100.

was made a few days after Booth's. This time the victim was a
more irregular attender of the same society's meetings, an
Irish weaver of the name of Thomas Dunn. Dunn was a creature of very unsettled habits, who had led a roving life and even
during his two years in Manchester had five or six different jobs.
During the autumn of 1792 he had drifted in to the societies'
meetings, mainly for the free warmth and company which he
found at Walker's house. On other evenings, being very fond
of the bottle, he was often found completely tipsy in the ale-
houses of the town.

Mr. Griffith must have rubbed his hands when Dunn was
picked up by his men, in the act of giving away seditious
literature. Here was a fellow of no real loyalties, who could
probably be induced to swear almost anything, provided he
had had enough to drink. Mr. Griffith laid on the liquor: Dunn
was liberally supplied with "shrub" (strong Holland's gin)
from the day of his arrest, and proved ready and willing to
supply any information required from his fertile Irish imagination.

It is somewhat curious to find that Thomas Dunn, who was
no hero, still less a would-be martyr, should have been distributing the "peace" leaflet a few days after Booth's arrest of 7th
June, of which he must have known. Perhaps he had drunk
himself into a state of bravado; perhaps—and possibly more
likely—a strain of cunning had prompted him to get taken up
by the constables, as the safest course, at a time when it was
not beneficial to be a Jacobin, but extremely profitable to give
information against them. At any rate, he seems to have been
very ready to oblige the constables who made his arrest, and
who gave the following account of it:

"On Tuesday night, the 11th June, a man [Dunn] was taken
into custody for distributing papers in a public house, intitled
War and signed Sydney. . . . One Callaghan was present and
said Dunn was a notorious Rogue and Democrat; and made a
common practice of delivering such papers.

"The next morning Dunn . . . was taken to the office of the
Magistrates' Clerk, where on being informed of the charge
against him he took the Constable aside, and told him to go to
his house, and that, under the bed, quite up to the wall, at the

back of an old box, he would find a handkerchief with some books tyed in it." The constables went, and found, "in the situation Dunn had described, several pamphlets and publications, of books read at the Reformation Society. At this time Dunn was much intoxicated and sayed he would tell everything he knew, but he was put by until the afternoon, and when he had recovered himself, he was examined and gave his first information which was read to him. . . It was read over several times, he sayed it was right."[1]

Among other accusations, made on oath, against the democrats Dunn swore that Booth had cursed the King, and wished "it was in his power he would guillotine him"; also that he had lent Dunn the "Address to the Addressers" (which Booth later reported to have been taken by the Irishman from his house, without permission, a few days before the arrest).

On the strength of this, Booth was confronted by the constables again, the very night he had got home; he was taken back to the prison, where the taskmaster, William Robinson, told him that Dunn had been brought in, dead drunk, a little earlier. While Booth was confined in a narrow cell, however, Griffith had given orders that "Dunn should lie in a good bed, have whatever he pleased, and go wherever he chused within the gates, and be treated with all the civility he could be".

Dunn's information had, in the meanwhile, been sent up to London for the perusal of the Lord Chancellor, the Attorney-General, the Home Secretary, and others in whose hands the fate of so many honest Radicals at that time lay. Their victims of the Manchester Societies were in a sorry pass, scattered, isolated, many of them arrested, all anxious.

Walker himself was extremely worried. He had gone to London on business early in June, and there the news reached him not only of Booth's arrest, but that a rumour was going about that he was to be served with a warrant for high treason.

He had expected some sort of charge to be brought against him, but had never imagined that he would be accused of a crime which was punishable by the death penalty! It would have been laughable, if he had not known the bitterness of his enemies' hatred; but even with this knowledge it seemed quite

[1] Treasury Solicitor's Papers 3505.

incredible, and he waited impatiently for confirmation or denial. What he heard from Manchester was not reassuring: Samuel Jackson, secretary of the Constitutional Society, had lost his wife, through illness brought on by these worries, and on the day of her funeral the constable followed him to the graveside, to arrest him immediately after the burial. The Reverend John Griffith told Richard Walker, some time later, "that he wished Unite not to interrupt the ceremony as that would be rather indelicate—but to take him up as he returned home".[1]

On 14th June, William Paul, a member of the Reformation Society, had been arrested on Griffith's warrant, charged with high treason "by compassing the death of his present Majesty" on the sole word of Thomas Dunn; he was kept in the New Bailey for ten days. After which, he was transferred to Lancaster Castle till the August assizes (being unable to get bail as this is forbidden in a treason case), for "though it required two men to convict a man of High Treason, one only was sufficient to have him *committed*".

Oliver Pearsall, a weaver, and James Cheetham, a hatter (also Reformation Society members) arrested on the same baseless charge, suffered the same fate. The authorities' hatred for the democrats was so intense that they were particularly badly treated: in Cheetham's case, for instance, "although there was a vacant bed in the room where he lodged the night of his arrival at Lancaster, he was removed into another room the night after, where he was obliged to sleep either upon the floor, or in the same bed with the common hangman". Paul had to sleep "in one of the cells of the fellons" with no glass in the windows—as result of which he contracted pneumonia and a violent inflammation of the eyes.[2]

While these torments were being inflicted on some of the societies' members, others—McCallum, Smith and Barrett—managed to escape to America, fortunately for them, as Dunn had sworn that they too had "cursed the King and wished to guillotine him". And what Dunn said, was good enough for the authorities, it seemed.

Walker heard all this, and it did not increase his peace of

[1] Appendix to Walker Trial.          [2] Ibid.

mind. He was still in London in August, for it was obviously not safe to return to Manchester at that moment. He did what he could to make the shocking case of Booth and Paul known to prominent people in London; he told the story of Booth's detention to the Society of Constitutional Information, who passed a resolution of protest; he wrote to friends when Paul was at last released, half-blind and penniless, asking them to help by buying his hats: "There is a poor honest *persecuted* democratic Hatter, who is indicted along with me," he writes to young James Watt, "to whom orders for about £60 to £100 from ready money customers would be particularly serviceable; he can send the same articles and at the same prices as the rest of his neighbours; I know you will take pleasure in serving this poor fellow, and I will be answerable for the execution of any orders you may send him; he has made me the best Hat I ever had in my life. . . ."[1]

*        *        *

But to return to Booth, languishing in the New Bailey after his second arrest; he found soon enough that he was there for a long stay this time, and for a very horrible reason.

Griffith, Parker (the Magistrate's clerk) and Hardman, the constable, had decided that he was to be the second witness needed to convict Thomas Walker of high treason.

Booth wrote afterwards to Walker, giving the whole story of how they gradually broke down his resistance by blackmail, bullying and threats. What mainly overcame him was the warning that his family would suffer if he did not do what was demanded of him—not to mention the repeated predictions of his gaolers that he himself would be hanged.

He was told among other things that three others had joined in evidence with Dunn, and that "I had but a few hours to determine whether I would suffer myself or save from infamy and destruction my three children, my wife and myself, and leave those whose property would defend them, to take care of themselves".

The taskmaster "begged I would save myself and said all the town would respect and support me". Booth however still

---

[1] Walker-Watt Correspondence.

firmly denied Walker's saying he would like to guillotine the King—which was one of Dunn's choicest pieces of evidence.

Many questions were shot at him, to get him to incriminate Walker and Paul. On one occasion Griffith told him "he wanted the great men; he wanted to pick his birds". (Booth noticed that the reverend gentleman "seemed to be intoxicated".) He said he was sure Booth "knew more, and he, Griffith, would not be trifled with", though, as poor Benjamin wrote, "I said more than what was true," and "was left to a night of the greatest anguish of mind I ever had experienced".

Day after day, the questioning went on, Booth gradually giving way and agreeing to more and more false testimony put into his mouth by Griffith. At last his pardon was sent for, and by then, "seeing me so zealous in their cause, I was ordered to board with the Taskmaster, to have a moderate allowance of drink, but not to make Dunn jealous". This was Mr. Griffith's order; and it seems that Dunn "drank all day"—beginning very early with a bottle of shrub at the clergyman's house, and a bottle of sherry at Paynter's.

In spite of Booth's promotion, however, Griffith was still complaining, on 17th June, that the prisoner was screening Walker. The magistrate tried to break down the last vestiges of Benjamin's resistance, by saying "that they did not want to take Walker's life, but something which would subject him to fine and imprisonment; as they knew it was him and others like him who had led the ignorant astray". He urged Booth to "declare what would be thought sufficient to form an evidence for the Crown".

On 18th June, Booth tells us, "a person was come down, sent for the purpose by Government, to examine Dunn's evidence, and hear what I had to say. . . . The Taskmaster said . . . if I did not declare to the full extent of my knowledge, I most certainly should be hanged, as my pardon was denied. . . . Upon the account I gave, my life depended."

Now really rattled, Booth "applied to Dunn to know what evidence he had given". It must have been something of a shock to hear the long and fantastic account of seditious activities practised by the societies, including "learning the manual exercise to assist the French should they land", and other sensational occupations, the truth of which Booth was asked to corroborate.

"The person spoke of" (who, we learn later, was Mr. Shelton, an agent from the Home Office) then appeared with Griffith, and examined Dunn, and while he was doing so, the Task-master and Parker, the clerk, exhorted Booth again "for God's sake and my family's, to join Dunn's evidence". The poor fellow was called before "the person", who "said he thought I should be tried, but if I chose to say anything, he would take it down; but it would neither do me good nor harm".

In the end Benjamin broke down, and said what he was expected to say . . . "Which," as he seems to sob out to Walker, in his account, "if it never appears I hope my friends will excuse my relating, and if it ever does, I declare it was the extorted efforts of a poor man to save himself and family, as I thought then, from shame and misery . . .". He adds that "I almost blessed my imprisonment, and I am convinced it was the Almighty's doing, that I might acquaint my friends of what they were accused; and by having alone stuck to truth in the minutes I have penned, I hope the counsel for myself and friends will be able to defeat these vile machinations".[1]

There is no doubt that it was an advantage to Walker and the rest of the accused to be informed of what was going on against them; but the price paid by Booth in physical and mental agony was terribly high. His troubles did not end even with his release. For the authorities responsible for his purgatory, revealing a staggering cynicism and sadism, had him re-arrested almost immediately, and charged with "having damned the King" on the sole testimony of Dunn; and although the latter was flatly contradicted by Booth's sister, who was present when the words were said to have been uttered, Benjamin was found guilty, at the Manchester Sessions of July, 1793, and sentenced to twelve months' imprisonment in Lancaster Castle. At the same time, he was again indicted on the charge of "conspiracy" which was being brought against ten members of the popular societies by the Crown. He was thus deprived even of the consolation he had hoped for, to give

[1] Walker, *Review*, pp. 101-9.

I

public evidence "of the practices made use of . . . to prevail on me to give false testimony".

To top his misery came a letter from the pastor of his church on 27th September: this accused him of "bringing a scandal on that sound branch of the Catholic Church of which you are a member", and reminded him "that unfeigned allegiance to your Sovereign is an essential doctrine and duty of Christianity, and that all coercive resistance to him is threatened with Damnation". The pastor, Mr. Cartwright, exhorted Booth to reform himself "and leave the rest to God. Whoever attempts to reform his superiors and the governing powers by the arm of flesh will only fall from one wickedness to another." He concluded: "You lie under the censure of the GREATER EXCOMMUNICATION" and "without an EXEMPLARY REPENTANCE there can be NO PARDON FOR YOU EITHER IN THIS WORLD OR THAT WHICH IS TO COME". By "exemplary repentance" he means "disclosing to a proper magistrate everything which you know of seditious and rebellious plots . . . and endeavouring to bring all your associates in iniquity to such punishment as the law prescribes". The letter is signed, "your faithful but afflicted pastor and friend".[1]

Walker has not recorded whether Booth publicly retracted the false evidence forced from him while in prison in June, or whether, after being convicted of sedition himself, he was no longer considered a suitable witness against Walker; the charge of high treason was dropped, Dunn being the only effective witness. In spite of every effort, nobody could be found to support Dunn: even Callaghan (who hobnobbed with him in the public houses), a good-for-nothing loafer, ready enough to sell his soul in the ordinary way, declared that, in this matter of giving evidence against Walker, "he would have done had it gone only to fine and a little imprisonment, but that when he found there was meant to be blood in the case he would have nothing to do with it". Callaghan, in spite of appearances, seems to have been a man of higher principles than some in the Privy Council and Law Courts, who were not at all averse to the idea of hanging Thomas Walker, on evidence fair or faked.

\*　　　\*　　　\*

[1] Appendix to Walker Trial.

Booth's story was corroborated for Walker by someone who knew Griffith; among other things he was told by the magistrate "that Dunn was a long time before he would say anything, but that he (Griffith) out with a decanter of shrub and made the dog drunk, and then he began to open; that he showed him (Dunn) his examination when he came to himself, and that he always stood to it since".

The reverend gentleman also declared "that he would not leave Walker a pair of shoes—he would ruin him". On another occasion he also declared his readiness to stab Walker, and said that he would hang him if possible.

That Dunn lived well while in gaol is shown by a copy of the bill for his board from 13th June to 6th August which was presented to Rev. John Griffith by the Taskmaster of the prison. "Board wages" cost his hosts £7 17s., and there was a long catalogue of wine, porter and small beer for him and his wife, consumed on top of the plentiful free drinks provided by Griffith and Paynter.

The account was paid by Mr. Simpson, in Brown Street, "Treasurer of an Association for preserving Constitutional Order and Liberty, as well as Property against the various efforts of Levellers and Republicans, entered into at Manchester, the 11th day of December 1793".[1]

The Association were being involved in considerable expense for the privilege of ruining Thomas Walker. But very possibly expense was no object to them. And although their contribution had not been successful in ensuring Thomas's trial for high treason, it had helped in establishing evidence for a charge of conspiracy—Dunn's own unaided testimony being sufficient for this. With an increase of anti-French, pro-war propaganda during the next few months, they could allow themselves to feel hopeful of a verdict of Guilty, which would crush Walker and put him permanently out of action in civic life, commerce and politics.

[1] Walker, *Review*, pp. 116-19.

## CHAPTER XIII

## SUSPENSE (1793, Summer)

DURING the first few months of the war, things went from bad to worse for the British—as indeed they continued to do for several years. The chance of stamping out the Revolution by a swift combined move on Paris was missed; the First Coalition was a dismal failure. Thousands of lives of British troops were muddled away in Flanders and eaten up in the poisonous swamps of the West Indies, which were turned into a battlefield because of their vital concern to the City interests.

The defeats of the Allied armies were very poor recruiting propaganda, and there was widespread desertion from the forces.

In Lancashire, for instance, in spite of leaflets and posters offering every inducement to join up, including an allowance to the recruit of "as much grog as he could drink", there were long lists of deserters in the Manchester newspapers of the period.

At the same time, the unemployment and poverty at home, foretold by the Radicals, were increasing rapidly. Various palliatives were tried in Manchester, such as substituting short-time for the workers instead of mass dismissals, giving food instead of wages, and so on. The *Chronicle* reports on 4th May that "greatly to the honour of many of the Manufacturers in this town they have exerted themselves to assist the distressed weavers and others by *giving them a part of the work they have been used to receive*. Others have adopted the plan of buying bacon, cheese, potatoes, etc., and distributing them out to work-people on a Saturday instead of money, thereby serving them in the most essential manner. But notwithstanding this humane assistance there are numbers of the working class whose situations are truly distressing, and for whose relief some means should be suggested." Mr. Wheeler, the Editor, anti-Jacobin as he was, had to admit that "the commerce of this country must be supported. It is the vital system of its existence and cannot be materially injured but ruinous consequences will follow. Such a shock as the present is scarcely in memory, and we trust the cause of it will never return."

On 13th June, the *Chronicle* again reveals the anxiety of the Manchester business men: "Wednesday's *Sun* tells us of the flourishing state of commerce and the perfect restoration of credit and confidence and the great plenty of money in London.

"There is no circumstance we should be happier in subscribing to, but we must say it is not so in the country—though we trust the times will ere long change for the better."

By 21st December the state of things was so bad that an ardent Church and King man, John Greenwood, wrote to the *Chronicle* observing that "the trade of this once flourishing town has received such an alarming shock that men no longer hesitate in pronouncing it to be caused by war. . . . We have gained inconsiderable successes; as a dreadful blow against us, we have made the French unanimous amongst themselves. Gentlemen, the present stagnated state of the trade of this place calls aloud for your speedy and effective assistance."

Greenwood's remedy, however, was not likely to be very effective: "Forget all party differences. Put aside all private pique. Lay your grievances at the foot of the Throne. The Father of his people will not refuse to hear them. . . ."

Unfortunately, neither the King nor the King's ministers had any cure to offer during the disastrous early months of the war, except increased persecution of those who had wanted to prevent hostilities and who still pressed for peace negotiations. They were labelled as traitors, and the virulence with which Booth, and Cheetham, and Paul were maltreated was due, in some measure at least, to the resentment of their oppressors at the French successes, and at the strength of the anti-war feeling in Manchester.

It was of course not only in Manchester that the hot breath of persecution was felt. The London societies were suffering acutely from the witch-hunt, and membership had fallen rapidly in both the Constitutional Information Society and the Corresponding Society. However, they continued to carry on considerable activity, mainly in collecting signatures to petitions for electoral reform.

The minutes of the L.C.S. show the untiring efforts of its members to get signatures. "3rd April: Resolved to send circular letter. Small Bills to be stuck up *in the night*, informing the Public where the Petition lays. Mr. Francis to be requested to present the Petitions."—"15th April. The Business of Delegates last night only collecting numbers of signatures—3500"; and "Deputations to request Mr. Fox to present ye Petitions. Fifield, Gerrald, Margarot . . . have been several times and cannot see him."

Gerrald seems to have been particularly energetic; there is a minute to the effect that "he took his skin [the parchment form] to the King's Bench Prison and got two hundred signatures there". When the forms were gathered in, ready for presenting, "some of the skins were very dirty, blotted and marks of a X for a name":[1] it did not matter; they all added to the great pile that was presented on 6th May, by the Whig member, Francis.

Fox had been asked to present the petitions, but he pointed out that it would not be appropriate, as he was an opponent of universal suffrage. He did, however, support the motion for the consideration of the petitions by a committee, in a speech forcefully pointing out the need for reform. "The time must come when the House would be unable to disguise even from themselves the necessity of inquiring into the state of the representation of the people." He quoted, in condemnation of the procrastinating Tories, the mediaeval verse:

> Let that be wrought which Mat doth say,
> Yes, quoth the Erle, but not to-day.

In spite of Fox's effort and a brilliant speech by Grey exposing the corruption of the electoral system, and the recent heavy increases in taxation, the motion was lost by 282 to 41.[2]

With the defeat of the petitions, and the object lesson that it was no use asking a rotten parliament to cure itself, the Corresponding Society turned to straightforward methods to gain their objectives; they held large open-air meetings, and planned a great national convention. There was an uncomfortable feeling in the air that things would get worse before they got

[1] Treasury Solicitor's Papers, 3504.    [2] *Collected Speeches of Charles James Fox.*

better; and though public meetings, dinners and so forth were allowed, and the leaders moved about and spoke openly enough, the smaller fry were being caught in the closing net, and it was clear that sooner or later the big fish would be threatened.

Thomas Walker felt the atmosphere keenly, and found the suspense of his own position intolerable. He went to London to arrange his affairs, and wrote, from Bates Hotel in the Adelphi, to Mr. Dundas, the Home Secretary, asking him to deny or confirm "a report industriously circulated in Manchester of a charge of HIGH TREASON made against me". He excused himself for taking up Dundas' time "with the frivolous rumours that idle and ignorant, or bigotted and malevolent people may amuse themselves with propagating at the expence of my character". But he says that "the report is in itself so serious, and has been the topic of so much conversation at Manchester, that I think it right . . . to obviate any *false construction* which my enemies may put upon my absence from home, to inform you, Sir, that my residence is as above mentioned, and that I shall not merely be *ready and willing* but *desirous* to meet any charge that may be made against me from whatever quarter it may proceed . . .".

Receiving no answer from Mr. Secretary Dundas, he wrote again, saying he supposed "the intent of the charge was not to punish me for a political offence, of which I know I am not guilty, but to injure my general character and reputation indirectly indeed, but irrevocably".

"The character and credit of a commercial man, Sir, is too delicate to be trifled with," he insists. "Hitherto, mine has been unsullied; and I trust it will remain so by any conduct of my own. But the principle of harassing a British merchant by vague reports, industriously circulated, of crimes he has never committed, by charges unfounded and threats unexecuted, is so base, so detestably malignant, that I hope, for the honour of the national character, that it is confined to my enemies at Manchester." Walker believes that the secretary of state must know of any such criminal charge, and entreats that "I may be kept no longer in suspense . . . and my mind set at ease, so that I may be enabled to attend to my commercial concerns, without the perpetual anxiety attendant upon reports and suspicions most injurious and unfounded".

On 16th July, Dundas had still not replied. Mr. Wharton, Whig member for Beverley, who had delivered the last letter, assured Thomas that Dundas had read it in his presence, "and said that it was impossible for him [Dundas] to make any other reply than that he had received serious and criminal charges against you . . . and had taken such steps as his official duty required to have those charges investigated . . .".

Wharton told Walker that he had remarked to Dundas that "personal enmity to you [Walker] and jealousy of your commercial connections had instigated persons who had failed in their attempts to injure you commercially, to make this attempt to take away your life". To which Dundas replied evasively that "it was very possible that there might be low and personal motives for the prosecution, and that he had too good an opinion of your understanding to suppose you would subject yourself to the penalties of high treason".

Walker waited till 29th July, when, still being without any written word from Dundas, he wrote a third letter to him, saying he was "induced to expect an early intimation of the intended proceedings against me, or of their having been relinquished".—"I should be much surprised," he added, "that no decision had yet taken place on this business, if I were not conscious that the more strictly the accusations were investigated, the more futile they would appear."[1]

Still no answer. For the very good reason, that, as Thomas suspected, nobody had been able to make a case of any sort against him, let alone a convincing one.

Of course Dundas knew all about it; Mr. Shelton, the clerk of the Arraigns, had been sent to Manchester, certainly with his knowledge, to take depositions; he was, as we know, "the person" who examined Booth.

Walker learned later that Shelton stayed, on that occasion, with Nathaniel Milne, the viciously anti-democrat magistrate, and that he had told Milne that "he blamed Mr. Griffith very much and made a report of Dunn's evidence by no means favourable to the further proceedings against us".

[1] Appendix to Walker Trial.

Mr. Griffith confessed, indeed, "that they could not convict Walker of high treason now, because they had lost the evidence of Booth, who was bailed, and they had only one witness; but as they had begun he thought they should go on".

Mr. Milne "was heard to observe that it was very extraordinary indeed that, although he had a list of several hundred Democrats, he could not procure another evidence".[1]

In London, while Walker was writing to Dundas, Dundas was writing to the Lord Chancellor, to Sir John Scott (the Attorney-General) and others, to discover whether they thought it safe and profitable to proceed with the Walker prosecution. Mr. Shelton gave his opinion in a report of 25th June, and very deprecating it was: "Dunn contradicts the most material parts of his former information, and in such a manner that, together with his being a drunken and very seditious fellow himself, I thought it not prudent to take any steps on it without further directions."

He goes on to say that "I should have brought two warrants with me against Walker but (for reasons I will mention later), I declined doing so. . . . Booth was extremely desirous to say everything he knew. . . . Dunn is not very intelligent and I am apprehensive he has been tampered with. If his first information had been received privately, and he had been committed a close prisoner, considerable discoveries might have been made perhaps on searching Walker and Paul's houses, but the business had been noised all over the town and neighbouring county, and Paul has been arrested and committed last week, so that there had been sufficient time to destroy or remove any papers which either of them were desirous should not be discovered. . . ." The envelope of this letter is marked "read by Lord High Chancellor; by William Pitt; by Lord Grenville".

Sir John Scott and Sir John Mitford wrote to Dundas on 19th July, giving their considered opinion "of the nature of the offence with which Walker is charged", from what they had seen of the documents of the case.

"We think," they write, "these papers contain a state of circumstances which amount to a high misdemesnor; but it does not appear to us that they impute a crime of a higher nature."

[1] Walker, *Review*, p. 121.

They think "it would be impossible by any evidence which the papers lead us to imagine can be produced, to convict Mr. Walker of such crime. Whether he could be effectually prosecuted upon a charge for a misdemesnor must depend upon the credit which a jury could be induced to give to the persons whose informations have been transmitted to us" [Dunn, Griffith, Booth]. "This will be seen by prosecutions now depending . . . when some of the persons mentioned must be given credit. If such credit be not given, we do not think charge of misdemesnor against Mr. Walker can be supported."[1] The prosecutions referred to included that of Booth; one can hardly believe that Dunn's evidence there would have much credit, except to prove his own drunkenness; as for instance when asked: "Was you drunk when you fully resolved to turn informer?" he answered: "No. After I turned informer I got pretty forward in liquor; at most times I am fond of liquor."[2]

In spite of all the grave doubts in the most learned legal minds of the country, somebody was out for blood and determined to go ahead with the carnage, come what might. One small portent was a handbill which was sold in the Manchester streets during the late summer, headed. "Some PARTICULARS relating to a NEW DISCOVERY which contains an Account of the Accomplices of Tom Paine's journeymen, who were taken by warrant and committed to Prison on Friday last."

"The charges to be brought forward against them are, it is believed, of a very serious nature.

"The affair has caused much conversation in the town, and no small bustle with those concerned in it, as measures are pursuing that will bring the business to a speedy conclusion, and it is expected, to the satisfaction of the public at large. There is reason to suspect that the COOPER (who was lately in such full business) will now be out of employ; also the black cat be driven from the family [a reference to Samuel Jackson] and the two famous WALKERS (who are related to the above) will be shortly overtaken; and should either of these pedestrians meet with an antagonist whose abilities are superior, so as to hurry them from this stage of life, no expence will be spared to have them interred in a manner suitable to their character, as a

---

[1] Treasury Solicitor's Papers, 3498.          [2] Walker, *Review*, p. 113.

PAUL is already got, and a room is to be upholstered in black paper."[1]

It was quite obvious that the local Church and King Club and the Association men were set on going forward with the trial; the above handbill bears the stamp of their style. They financed Griffith for Dunn's stay in prison, as we have seen; they wrote a letter of congratulation to him "for his laudable exertions in bringing to justice all those who in any way offend against our most excellent form of Government", and thanked him because "through his activity . . . the factious crew of evil designing men, plotting to subvert our much admired Government and substitute Anarchy and Confusion have been entirely frustrated, and their vile and wicked designs brought to light".

Griffith himself, while no doubt delighted to have caused a stir in high places, and trouble and distress to the Walker family, seems to have been ill at ease about it; this appears from an account by Richard Walker, Thomas's younger brother, of an interview with the magistrate on 18th July, "in a public house in the church yard", when Griffith tried hard to evade the main issues. He admitted that "we cannot convict either Mr. Paul nor any other person of high treason, as we have only one witness".

Richard gave him Thomas's address on a card. "Mr. Griffith said I had better give the card to . . . Unite, who had the warrant and might do as he pleased. . . . He saw no reason for his [Griffith] acting; he had sent copies of information to the government, and could not tell why they did not act, and why they seemed to want to throw the business on a country justice"; he added, repeating himself, that they had only one witness, on which Richard commented that "with all the pains which it was reported he [Mr. Griffith] had taken, it was surprizing he could not get another witness as good as the one they had. . . ".

Mr. Griffith then said it was not incumbent on him to take any steps to apprehend Mr. Thomas Walker out of his own neighbourhood, to which Richard replied that "the warrant being for conspiring or compassing the death of the King, Mr. Walker being in London so near the King's person, he might

[1] Walker, *Review*, p. 110.

more easily have an opportunity of putting his wicked intentions into execution; and that it shewed little regard for the safety of the King to suffer those . . . accused of conspiring against his life, to be at large so near him without interruption".

Griffith protested that "he was persuaded that treason had been actually committed at Mr. Walker's house, but that Mr. Walker was not present at the time". Richard answered that "that was not a fact, as neither my brother nor I had any connection with people guilty of treason".

Mr. Griffith mentioned, in the course of this conversation that it "had been reported he had an indemnity from the government for what he had done, but that was not the case". However, we learn later that he declared he *was* indemnified by the government; "at one time, having only a verbal promise, he was very uneasy, but that he had obtained a written indemnification that morning".[1]

A month later, meeting Richard Walker again, Mr. Griffith asked him if Thomas would pledge himself to take his trial for *sedition* at the following assizes? "For," he said, "I have *two* charges against him, one for High Treason, and another for Sedition."

The reverend gentleman seems to have had a strange streak of simplicity in his queer and sinister character. He obviously preened himself quite openly on the success of his conspiracy, and his father, the Rev. Maurice Griffith, was equally gratified.

The latter "did not take a very public part" in all these proceedings, Thomas Walker tells us, "but he certainly did not take a very idle part; and he had been heard to declare, that if they (meaning his party) could but get Buller (meaning Judge Buller) down, they should get some of them (meaning myself and the other defendants) hanged".[2]

Such was the Christian spirit of this worthy gentleman of the Church.

---

[1] Appendix to Walker Trial.          [2] Walker, *Review*, p. 121.

## CHAPTER XIV

# BOYCOTT (1793-1794, Winter)

WALKER was being attacked on two fronts: the one political and personal, the other commercial and financial—more dangerous and more difficult to defend.

As we have seen, things were bad enough for anyone in business at this particular time, and although Walker's firm was as prosperous and solid as any in the country, it was not invulnerable to the growing dangers of depression and war; his enemies had good reason to hope that their campaign, added to the general crisis, would result in his downfall; and they spared no effort to ensure this.

We get a good idea of the troubles that began to beset him at this period from his prolific correspondence with James Watt, the son of the inventor, who had for about two years been employed by Walker as an assistant in the business, and was then travelling about the Continent, collecting credit and orders.

Both Thomas and Richard Walker were very fond of young Watt, who was a staunch member of the Constitutional Society, and had, as will be remembered, presented the famous address to the National Convention in April, 1792. This had much upset James Watt senior at the time, and caused a certain coolness between father and son, to the great regret of the Walkers and of Thomas Cooper, who was deeply devoted to young James and greatly admired his father.

James junior had not changed his opinions when he went abroad for the Walker firm in late 1792, but he realised the sense of Cooper's injunction: "You are going to Italy upon a business in which Walker's interest is much concerned—for yr sake and my sake and yr friends sake, talk no politics or religion," and wrote early in the year to Walker that he was determined "to remain neutral amongst the Parisian and Manchester democrats"—(to which Thomas replied "admiring his determination", and with, one can be sure, an indulgent and incredulous smile).

The Walkers' letters to young Watt extend over two years, and cover many subjects: the war and the political situation, local gossip, family matters; lengthy instructions on business matters alternate with recitals of personal troubles and worries, from friends' failures in business to Church and King plots.

Soon after the Manchester riots (30th December, 1792), Walker wrote to him that "public violence is over; but I almost hourly feel every species of malignity which it is possible either to devize or execute. The treatment I have met with I trust I have not deserved, and that I have protected not only my person and my property, but what is much dearer than either—my honor. . . ."

On 6th February he writes that "it is impossible to give you an idea of the rancour and malignity of the Aristocrats here, their folly you wd be convinced of from the paper which was inclosed in our last. I cannot stain my Paper with stating to you the baseness of some of their attempts, which are infamous and wicked beyond my powers of expression; conceive the worst you possibly can of them and your imagination will fall far short of what they wd accomplish if they could."

In spite of it all, his humour often prevails: as in a letter of 3rd March, 1793: "Yesterday being the anniversary of the Church and King Club to celebrate the victory...obtained over the Dissenters in their last appeal to Parliament for a Repeal of the Church and Test acts, it was to have been celebrated with more than usual splendour; at noon the Tories were to parade with the Committee for raising the Manchester Marine Corps, when just at the moment of their being ready to march, a Fire broke out in some new Buildings . . . which threatened much damage; this drew the public attention for some time; no sooner was the fire extinguished than it begun to rain; and in the evening when some thought they intended mischief, it began to blow one of the most furious hurricanes that have been experienced here for some years past; the consequence was that three Flags which these ignorant bigots had hoisted upon the old Church steeple were blown down and some of the Turrets along with them, which beat in the roof and damaged old Mother Church so that no service was performed to-day; all the old women in the Parish are dreadfully alarmed and regard the accident as ominous; a gentleman is this minute come in who says it is reported in the Town that I prayed for the wind to blow the Church down; if so they make me into a very righteous man, for my prayers were certainly heard. . . ."

But soon after this he was down in the depths of gloom again. His business was beginning to suffer, and there was no knowing how far it might deteriorate. There seemed no limits to the malice of his enemies: on 23rd July we read "that letters have been written into Italy with a view if possible to ruin us, we have no doubt; but by whom, or to whom we are ignorant; we have the information from one of the *first* Houses in this country, who though confident of the *fact* are not in possession of the proofs. Could they sink us I am confident they would; everything has been done that was possible to ruin us but thank God without effects; we have and shall, I have no doubt, baffle the utmost malice of all our enemies; amongst other reports it has been industriously propagated that I have been arrested by our Bankers here: the very reverse is the fact, for both . . . have behaved very kindly indeed . . ."

He repeatedly assures Watt of his faith in him: "Your exertions have been highly beneficial to us. . . . You will, I am confident, do all in yr power to discover who has endeavoured to ruin us in Italy. . . ." Writing on 16th February, Walker tells James: "Of this be assured, that you cannot serve us more, or more irritate and disappoint the Aristocrats than by selling our goods, settling our accounts, and sending us money, in all of which I am very confident you will have a double pleasure. . . . The rancour and malignity of our persecutors continues with unabated violence. . . ."

"Send us money" becomes a recurring theme: Thomas repeats, on 31st March, that "remittances come in very slowly indeed . . . you will ere this . . . have collected and transmitted us some considerable sums—which will be extremely welcome and enable us to fulfil our engagements with that punctuality which will baffle and confound our *amiable* enemies".

Perhaps owing to dirty work on the part of these enemies, "the mode in which many of the Houses at Naples conduct themselves is extremely unpleasant. It appears that Javanet has paid only £115 towards our draft of £131 16s. 2d. of the 6th November, and that Della Camera . . . have neglected to provide for our drafts on them payable in Leghorn. . . ." Speaking of goods going to Ancona, Naples, Genoa and Leghorn (3rd April), "Your presence in Italy is indispensably necessary till they are disposed of . . . ."

In this same letter, Walker says "the Distress of this country is by much greater than you can imagine, many of the labouring poor are out of employ, what will become of them God only knows . . .".

The labouring poor, as we already know, were suffering terribly. So in a lesser degree, but still substantially, were the small businessmen, who included many of Walker's Radical friends; Thomas Cooper wrote to Watt on 7th April that "the want of confidence here (produced first by the Proclamation and then by the War) has been the cause of procuring difficulty so singular, so deep, so general that a universal Bankruptcy is threatened". He tells him that his firm, Joseph Baker and Company, has failed: the creditors meet on Wednesday. "We shall probably have a large surplus. But time we must have. The trouble, the anxiety, the exertion and the fatigue mental and bodily that we have all had for two months past is beyond description."

He mentions four or five firms who "have been compelled to do what we have been compelled to do. In fact everybody is in want: not merely in want but in Danger." Walker confirms this on 3rd April: "The storm which I have long foreseen is now beginning to rage with fury; my friend Cooper and Joseph Baker & Co I fear will fall victims to it; a statute of Bankruptcy was sent for on Monday last . . . this information I know will grieve you to the soul, as our poor friend, I much fear, will have very little mercy shewn him. . . ."

Cooper's next two letters to young Watt give more details; his firm has had to go into liquidation: "The Creditors have proposed of their own accord to allow us three years to pay our debts in" (24th April). He reports other "failures": "Since my last, Jones the banker has stopped payments, and I have heard to-day that Heywood had. . . ." He goes on, "I believe Walkers will stand: God in Heaven grant they may; I am superstitious about them."

On 7th April he writes that "the kindness of the Walkers to us has been what you wd suppose & what we shd expect from our best and dearest friends". And indeed Walker, though much oppressed himself, did what he could for Cooper, raising a loan of £6,000 "part of which we borrowed from Jones, and the remainder from Tuffin of Warrington; 2,000 we must repay immediately, and the remaining 4,000 upon the first day of June next".

It was obviously not easy for Thomas to find the money: "I need not say, when coupled with the bare and illiberal treatment which we have met with, and with all the embarassing circumstances of the present time (of which you can furnish evidence) it will be particularly inconvenient to us; notwithstanding, unless *our own resources* fail us very materially, we should weather the Storm, violent as it is, and defeat the utmost efforts of party malevolence. . . . With regard to our loan to Cooper, we have a good deal of security in our hands, and I am not apprehensive of much (if any) eventual pecuniary loss; but the engagement will certainly be of no service to us, indeed we had this day a very unpleasant application made to us, in consequence of our having entered into it." (3rd April, 1793).

Cooper was very much concerned about the Walkers' business: "It is impossible they can avoid feeling (tho' not as we do) the present evil." He adjures Watt to do his utmost for them: "You are now more than ever necessary to the Walkers, for in you they can place unlimited confidence, as to Integrity and Ability." He warns him against believing well of people too hastily. "I know you will pardon me this, for the Interest I take in what you do in all that concerns the Walkers; to whom the most rascally & detestable public of Manchester have behaved most infamously." The "very unpleasant application" mentioned by Walker is here explained: "He (Walker) was arrested *in the open Market place* on yesterday week by Nat Milne at the suit of Hall the dyer for about £900, & my supposed Absence from England . . . assigned as a Reason!" It was not just fear of not being paid that made Mr. Milne so assiduous in humiliating the merchant.

K

Cooper urges Watt, "my dear friend, stay in Italy, return to Naples sell at short Credit & remit early to the Walkers. . . . Half Manr is or will be insolvent; we who have stopt payment are almost regarded as prodigies of punctuality; you are now more wanted than ever. God bless you & write often."

In the same letter, Cooper tells Watt that he is "resolved to quit Trade. . . . My friends wish me (I think stupidly) to follow the Law; my own wish is to live while I can, & therefore if I can muster 1000£ or 2000£ I will endeavour to persuade my wife to accompany me to America." A fortnight later, he repeats that "for my own part I mean (if I can) to beg about 500£ and go to America. . . . Tuffin & Sharp are violent for my going again to the bar; so is Mrs. C. but I feel a most inveterate disinclination to live upon my friends for 3 years & work like a Negro for ten years more. In America I can yet do even as a farmer. . . ." (24th April.)

Cooper stuck to his decision, and arranged to go and settle with Dr. Joseph Priestley. In August, 1793 he was due to leave, to prospect for both families, and there is a letter to young Watt, dated 24th August, Deal, written while "waiting in hourly expectation of the arrival in the Downs of the American Ship, the *Pigou*".

Cooper was anxious that the Walkers would emigrate too: "I hope," he writes on 24th April, "they will wind up their affairs and quit this most infernal and detestable kingdom." By the late summer he was very impatient to get off, as he was convinced that there would be a war between Britain and America, and had persuaded Priestley of this.

"Thomas (his son) is under the care of Priestley, who in consequence of the inevitable approach of an American War, has persuaded his wife to give her friends the slip and suddenly to go with him. So that he takes her and his children." Later, he writes, "I think the American war will blow up the whole system (in England) ere 6 months are over. Not that the Ministry care for the Commerce of the Country: on the contrary I am persuaded there is a serious premeditated intention to crush it, or at least most effectively to prune the wings of the commercial and manufacturing Interests as being too provoking and dangerous to the aristocracy of the Country. . . ."

This observation, though it was in fact wrong in point of time—for the war was not to happen—contained a good deal of insight; for the attitude of Pitt and his friends had not fundamentally changed since the days of the Fustian Tax battles.

Cooper's arguments carried weight with Walker, who had for some time been thinking of emigrating, and would probably not have hesitated but for his many commitments in England and his deep sense of duty to his country and its people. For several months he anxiously weighed the pros and cons. On 30th December he wrote to Watt that "I begin to have doubts whether this is the country for wise and honest men to live in; were I to consult my own interest or my own happiness I should quit it immediately; but which I will not do till I am thoroughly convinced that I can contribute less to the sum of human happiness in it than in any other; soon as I am convinced of that I will leave it to the Fools who may chuse to remain dupes to the Knaves who have the management of it". On 23rd January, he wrote "there is Virtue in the country or I am very much mistaken—if I am I will get out of it as soon as I can". But on 6th February, he says: "My present intention, is to leave this Country as soon as I can get my affairs settled and my property disposed of. . . ." On 16th February, after giving Watt instructions about business transactions, he asks him to "get here as soon as you can. . . . I am confident you can be extremely useful to us, particularly in the arrangements which it will be necessary to make previous to leaving this country, which I am absolutely determined to do, unless there should have been an alteration in the minds of the People, of which at present I can see scarcely a possibility; in the state which this country at present is, no Man will stay in it who is not either a fool or a Knave. You will not be left. America in my opinion is the country to go to; my wife, who behaves nobly, is as willing to go as I am. . . ."

In another letter, dated also 16th February—after thanking young Watt for the olives he sent, of which some have been posted to Cooper, Priestley, Hawkes and Ferriar—he repeats his plan "to contract our business and to settle our affairs— that in case affairs here should not mend, I at least with my family may go to America upon which we are much bent".

On 12th August, Cooper writes at Walker's request: "The intention of T.W. is to wind up his Concerns as quickly as possible, and . . . to leave this detestable Country. But as this can only be done gradually, and as the goodwill of a Business which has cost so much time and trouble and money is too serious an object to be thrown away, T.W. and R also mean to execute with redoubled punctuality every order of every house worth preserving, and to regain that Credit which you intimate they once had, and have not kept up of late times. It wd be cursedly embarassing to have complicated or litigated accounts to settle, if they were ready to go in the course of a year or two. T.W. certainly means to go, and to America. R.W. talks with equal inclination of going to France."

On 30th October, Thomas was still undecided. "Whether I shall stay in this Country is very doubtful, if I do there must be a very great and material alteration indeed, and that very soon; but I shall not act at all unless a very different disposition manifests itself in the People; if they chuse to starve with Church and King in their mouths, for me at least they shall. . . ."

But he had to abandon any hopes of emigrating, at least temporarily. Instead of making preparations for a voyage to to America he had to put all his energies into preparing for the trial which was being mounted against him.

He had been forced earlier in the summer to stay away from home for about three months; in Cooper's words (12th August, 1793) "because the rascals at Manr. wish to execute upon him a warrant for high Treason (compassing the death of the King!) at Manchester, whence he would be hurried to Lancaster and kept there, instead of executing it in London where he wd be committed to Newgate and be visited by his friends". Cooper added that "all this is more aimed at his commercial than political Reputation".

In London Walker in fact found plenty to do; he wrote his letters to Dundas, he got into touch with Thomas Erskine, the brilliant Whig who agreed to conduct his defence; he attended dinners and meetings of the L.C.S. and the Constitutional Society, where he met his friends, among them Felix Vaughan and Thomas Lloyd, who also promised to act as counsel for the

defence; he sat for his portrait to George Romney; he attended
as well as he could to his business, but seems to have had little
time to write the usual long letters of instructions to young
Watt. It was from Cooper that Watt learned, on 24th August,
that "the Prosecutions against Paul and Walker for Treason
are dropt; the former has been confined near 3 months in
Lancaster Gaol upon the charge, & the latter in Jeopardy of
the same situation . . . for nearly the same length of time".
From the same letter, Watt heard of the indictment for sedition
and conspiracy and about Booth's trial: "Mr. Benjamin Booth,
a ci-devant servt of Walker has been convicted at Man.
sessions last week for cursing the King, upon the suborned
evidence of one Dunn, ci-devant secretary of the Patriotic
Society who has been made drunk and threatened out of his
senses and his honesty. . . . Lloyd (counsel for the defence) did
not succeed. The brutes of Manr. clapped and applauded
Topping when he was opening the charge. Dunn is to be
evidence against Walker, who *ultimately* will triumph, but his
business is to get out from among the Scoundrels of this
rascally nation. . . ."

Richard Walker, writing on 17th August to young Watt,
tries to make light of the prospect of his brother's trial: "the
parties have been traversed till the next Assizes, when like the
rest of the Plots it will vanish *in fumo*. There is no doubt of their
getting off with honor and eclat, for independent of the charge
being unfounded it is so absurd and ridiculous that it will only
excite laughter in a Court of Justice."

But however sanguine the Walkers might be as to the result,
the last months before the trial were anxious and gloomy. On
top of all their business troubles, there were domestic sorrows;
in November, 1793 Richard lost his little boy from an attack
of chickenpox. He writes a very sad note, saying: "I have had
such pain in my head for several days and which I cannot get
rid of, that this must be very short. . . . Mrs. Walker bears the
heavy loss we have sustained with more fortitude than I expected. She was at Harrogate when the little boy was taken ill
and only returned the night before his Death."

History tells us little of such domestic tragedies, and we
can only guess at the personal hardships of their families.

Thomas just occasionally reveals their reactions to the ordeal, as when he remarks: "my two eldest girls behaved with great firmness, and Tom, upon being insulted by two Boys in the street acted with a degree of courage and propriety far beyond what could be expected from one of his years". The father adds that "reflections like these cause emotions to which the Aristo-crats are perfect strangers", (10th February, 1793).

The Walker children must inevitably have been affected by the tension and unusual activity of the household, as the trial approached. Their father was more and more harassed and pre-occupied, and although "my wife behaves like an angel" the strain for the family was very great. Young Watt would have been a great help and moral support to the Walkers who felt themselves surrounded by enemies, especially since Thomas Cooper's departure. Watt was due to return in the New Year of 1794, but Thomas, though impatient to see him, felt it would be very unwise for him to come back before the trial. There was a grave risk of his being arrested by Pitt's agents on account of his well-known sympathies with the French.

In spite of all Cooper's previous injunctions to him to be cautious and prudent, and "talk no politics or religion", James had not lost his youthful revolutionary ardour. The previous April, he had expressed his intention of joining the Republican forces, to Cooper, who, greatly upset, had written (10th April, 1793) an exasperated note telling him that "your notion of entering the French Army is a mad wildgoose scheme. You are by this time perhaps acquainted with the Treachery of Dum-ourier, and of the probable extinction of the French Republic; but whatever event had happened, none but the desperate shd go to the Army. You are not desperate. Jos Baker are not so. Less so are Walkers. . . . You have not lost yr Friends: & they have still need of you."

Now it seemed that Watt, although he had given up that plan, was still too ardent a republican not to defend his ideas when provoked; and it was reported in Lancashire that the young man had been spreading sedition while on his travels. He was said to have entered into political arguments when at Rouen some months back. He wrote to Walker on 12th Septem-ber, 1793, to find out what his accusers had said about him.

Walker answered, giving as much information as he could: (30th October) "From what I can learn the Person of whom Yates spoke is a Man of the name of Smallwood . . . now at Bordeaux, or in some other port of France; he is I believe the Fellow with whom you had some altercation at Rouen. He has lately been at Bolton, where I hear he has abused you without mercy; Jackson, who heard of his abuse at second hand, defended you in the manner you might expect. . . . Smallwood is your only enemy of whom I have yet heard"; Walker does his best to reassure Watt, but says, "to know what a persecutor means to *swear* in this country is no very easy matter".

He says he has asked the advice of the Radical lawyer Vaughan, "who is a very rising man at the Bar, and a sturdy Friend of Liberty". Vaughan "is inclined to think that a Man is not responsible in this Country for words said to have been spoken in another", but has promised "to consult his Books and send his opinion".

A few days later (3rd November) Walker writes that "so far from having heard that you ever held any discourses either at Paris or Rouen, or that you had given any advice whatever, I never heard a syllable of any such thing, or of any accusation against you till, in consequence of your letter . . . I made enquiries. . . . I have not heard a word more since; notwithstanding the falsehood, folly and meanness of your Accuser, I wd not by any means have you return till after my trial is over; *at this moment* your perfect innocence is a very sufficient ground with the Miscreants here, why you should be persecuted; you need no other crime; your return cannot serve me, but it is more than possible that it may be injurious to you. . . ".

Thomas would have been only too glad of Watt's presence and help, for he was overwhelmed with work; the preparation for the trial "almost engrosses the whole of my time . . . besides loading me with enormous expences impossible for me to avoid; circumstances . . . which afford great delight to the philanthropic minds of my amiable persecutors . . ." But in spite of his regrets and worries, his optimism breaks through: "No human consideration shall deter me from meeting the utmost malice of my enemies, over whom I hope finally to triumph, numerous and interested as they are; except poison and assassination, every machination possible for villainy to devize has been attempted to ruin and destroy me; thank God in vain." (30th October.)

The date of the trial was now fixed for 2nd April of the next year. During the remaining five months, Walker devoted himself to perfecting his defence. He had prepared to sub-poena Dundas if necessary; his witnesses were collected, and the lines of the defence had been worked out with Erskine, in whom he had implicit faith.

The main difficulty for them was the nebulous nature of the charge: "The offences I was charged with are sworn to have been committed between the third of November 1792 and the 12th of June 1793, which I understand is *all* the information I shall have from my Persecutors till I come into Court to be put upon my trial. . . . So much for British Justice." (30th October, 1793.)

Walker's complete innocence was, unfortunately, no weapon against the insidious network of lies and rumours which con-stituted the case for the prosecution; and he could not count on its value when it came to a matter of hard swearing in court, should the judge be an anti-Jacobin, and the jury packed with Church and King men. As he justly and bitterly observes, according to his experience "the most perfect innocence, at this moment, is no security against the wicked and villainous machinations of the enemies of freedom here".

## CHAPTER XV

## TRIAL (1794, Spring)

WALKER was not by any means alone in experiencing the law's delays and the failings of British justice under Pitt, nor the lack of security for even the most innocent. Anyone with Radical views or connections was liable to arrest and imprisonment. Men hardly dared open their mouths for fear some sentiment that could be construed as disloyal should escape them. As Cooper wrote to young James Watt, on 24th August, 1793, "Frost [a lawyer friend of the L.C.S.] is confined in Newgate for a twelvemonth for seditious expressions when he was drunk and sentenced also to be put in the Pillory. . . ".

It was not uncommon to be arrested, like Frost, in a public house for drinking a democratic-sounding toast; there were informers everywhere; friend reported on friend, servant on fellow-servant—as in the case of one Dinah Clarke, chambermaid to a gentleman in Croydon, who accused the gardener of calling the King "an Ass . . . and herself a 'wild Aristocrat' ".[1]

Government spies were busy infiltrating the meetings of the popular societies, following the members about, sending in full, flowery and often false reports to their employers in the Ministry. Correspondence was opened, and we find friends warning each other that their letters might be read. As early as December, 1792, Walker had written to James Watt, "I have great reason to believe that some of your letters are stopped; a meanness which I understand is now generally practised, and which prevents me from writing to you so fully as I could wish; not that I have anything to say that I care if all the world knew; but I do not chuse that a set of impudent and unprincipled Scoundrels shall pry into the Correspondence of warm and unreserved friendship."

And young James writing to his father from Naples, on 8th

[1] Treasury Solicitor's Papers 3495.

May, 1793, remarks that "many of the letters which I have written to Messrs Walker particularly upon the riots at Manchester and the riots at Rome in which I did not disguise my sentiments have been probably carried into Downing Street as they have never come to hand".

By the end of 1793 it was generally accepted that envelopes were opened; Thomas Hardy wrote to a correspondent asking him not to mention the L.C.S. on the address: "it was ten thousand to one that I received your letter". John Thelwall admonished Horne Tooke, about this time, to "seal your letters first with a Wafer and then some good Wax over it—You may as well stick your Letters together with your Spittle as use the Wax you generally have. It all rubs off in powder as soon as it is cold. Get good Wax! get good Wax! When Rogues and Robbers are in authority every Man ought to keep a good Lock upon his Door. . . ."[1]

In Scotland, Thomas Muir, brilliant young Edinburgh lawyer, and John Fyshe Palmer, the dissenting minister of Dundee, were tried in August and September, 1793, respectively, on charges of "sedition" and "seditious practices"—a description broad enough to convert any nonconformity into a crime against the state—and they were sentenced to seven years' transportation; many other trials were taking place every month and severe sentences were imposed on the slightest pretext.

One cannot help being astonished at the courage of the leaders of the popular societies. They were undeterred even by the grim punishments imposed by the Scottish court on Palmer and Muir, and they organised a National Convention, in Edinburgh during November, 1793, where representatives of many areas assembled to discuss a common plan of campaign for the coming months.

The events which took place during the Convention are well known, and so is the story of the trials that resulted, when Skirving, a Scot, and Gerrald and Margarot, the London delegates, were condemned to fourteen years' transportation for "conspiring to overthrow the State".

Tremendous indignation was aroused among the societies

1 Treasury Solicitor's Papers, 3495.

and their supporters by the news of the sentences, and meetings of protest were arranged early in 1794. On 11th January, soon after Margarot's trial, the L.C.S. held an anniversary dinner.

The toasts indicate the thoughts in all their minds: "The Rights of Man, and may Britons never want spirit to assert them", was the first; the second was to "Muir and Palmer, and may their sentences be speedily reversed, and Botany Bay peopled with *real* criminals". The third was to Maurice Margarot, "our condemned Delegate, with three times three".[1]

Not only the Radicals protested at the savage sentences; all decent opinion was shocked—and even unquestionably respectable persons in the House of Commons suggested that it was un-English and (though it might have happened in Scotland) could, and should, never happen here. The Government itself, in the trials of this period, though they might have preferred it otherwise, had to adopt constitutional and decent legal behaviour. Daniel Eaton, the popular publisher of *Politics for the People, or Hogswash* was acquitted, when tried for a seditious libel in February, and so were many other defendants especially in the London area.

Mr. Reeves, who acted as a sort of extra-official adviser to the Home Office, racked his brains to find a way of preventing these acquittals, and of making sure the democrats were caught and punished, by concocting a number of laws which would be infallible traps to anyone publishing or selling any anti-government material.

In a long report of April, 1794, he mentions several of the main difficulties of confounding his victims and stamping out sedition. "Law could deal with it [sedition] but the persons who give information could not be brought forward for fear of their lives. Some late acquittals and Ignoramuses have damped the hopes of repressing these evils in the course of Law as the Law now stands."

He thinks the juries are responsible in many cases "for certain recent acquittals", and says: "it is certain that some of them were occasioned by one or two of the personal friends of the defendants being on the Jury. Daniel Eaton dined with one of his Jury shortly before his trial, for instance." (Which shows

[1] Treasury Solicitor's Papers, 3495.

how carefully Mr. Reeves was watching the movements of our friends.)

In general, he goes on, "the Jury for Middlesex does not ... consist of the most *respectable* gentlemen, but of ordinary persons, who do not feel a pride in giving their best attention to the business of the county".—"It would be well," he thinks, "to consult with the chairman of the Sessions whether the Gentlemen of the County could not be prevailed on to resume the county business which they have so long neglected, because they thought it beneath them to attend at a Quarter Session."

He feels, however, that "disappointment over acquittal should not be suffered to deter from further prosecution", and suggests a variety of possible measures which could be taken, in the shape of new laws: "The disorders of the time require new remedies, and Laws made on the spur of the occasion have always been justified."[1]

One of the laws he thought of laid down that every pamphlet shop should be forced to have a licence—this to be granted by the local magistrates at their own discretion; thus the democratic booksellers would be effectively suffocated, as very few magistrates would be indiscreet enough to issue licences to known Jacobins.

The interest of Reeves' report is that, whether or not his suggestions were adopted, it seems to prove him to have been the chief adviser on these matters to the government. Sir Joseph Banks reinforces this impression in a letter to Dundas, on 22nd April: "Mr. Reeves and myself have frequently conversed on the subject of Mr. Thelwall's lectures, and we agree wholly in opinion that their tendency is dangerous in the extreme. My view is therefore well known to you who frequently consult that gentleman on police subjects. . . ."

Sir Joseph adds, referring again to Thelwall, that the latter "cannot fail frequently to utter sentiments which all moderate people will abhor—if so, a shorthand writer stationed upon him must in the course of a very few lectures provide matter against him from his own mouth sufficient to bring him to a jury with a moral certainty of conviction . . .".[2] In the light of what

---

[1] Treasury Solicitor's Papers, 3505.　　[2] Ibid., 3495.

happened when Thelwall was in fact brought before a jury, Sir Joseph's words have a certain dramatic irony.

On the one hand, intense police activity and Reeves' Associations at their busiest; and on the other, considerable life in the Corresponding Society (encouraged as it was bound to be by recent acquittals); a wave of anti-French feeling; and at the same time discontent at Pitt's government, owing to the increase in taxes and to wartime restrictions—these were among the elements that made up the background of Thomas Walker's trial, and gave him reason both for confidence and uneasiness.

Walker's personal reasons for anxiety were considerable; he knew from Richard's conversation with the Reverend Mr. Griffith that Thomas Dunn was the only witness against him, and so he could not be hanged for high treason; but he also knew that Dunn had sworn to fantastic accusations against him, which, if believed, would land him with a heavy sentence; he had heard what the Irishman had said, from Dunn's own lips, when one afternoon a fortnight before the trial he had come to Walker's house in a very tipsy state, full of penitence at his own wickedness, and bursting to tell Thomas all. He had asked to speak to Walker in private, but the merchant had refused, and the conversation took place before some friends of Walker's, including Mr. Seddon and Mr. Jones, both highly respectable Manchester solicitors.

In Mr. Seddon's words, "on being desired to speak, he repeatedly objected and declared he would say nothing before so many witnesses. . . . Mr. Walker refused [to have a tête-à-tête with Dunn] saying Dunn had sworn falsely against him; Dunn admitted that he had, and said that he had not had a quiet night for thirteen weeks. He then rose from his chair, and threw himself upon his knees and seized both Mr. Walker's hands and exclaimed with a great deal of emotion 'I have done you injustice and I beg your pardon.' He then cried excessively and addressing himself to Mr. Walker, said, 'My heart is broken . . . I have certainly done you wrong.'

"When Mr. Richard Walker (who was also present) asked 'who instigated you', Dunn answered, 'I am afraid to tell that . . . I have lodged an indictment against him but it is a damned

eternal falsehood.' At this stage he again cried very much and
threw himself down upon a table and was in an apparent agony
for about ten minutes. Thomas Walker said, 'You admit you
have done me an injury?' Dunn said, 'Yes, every person knows
it. . . . I will never go to Lancaster at the Assizes, let Griffith and
the rest of them do as they please and be damned.' Walker asked
again who instigated him? Dunn would not answer but cried,
'I know I behaved ill, I was bribed to do it, that is plump. But
I won't tell who did it, that shall for ever rest in my own
breast.' "[1]

Dunn did, in fact, try to avoid the assizes; but Walker sent
John Twiss, one of his workmen, to Preston to find him and
make sure he appeared in court. Dunn and Kinnaston, deputy
constable of Salford, were the only witnesses for the prosecution,
and had Dunn failed to appear, Walker would certainly have
been accused of having prevented him; a charge which he had
no desire to incur, being, on the contrary, anxious to see the
whole thing through now to the bitter end.

Having thwarted Dunn's attempt to evade the trial, Walker
was ready to face the music; as already mentioned, nobody had
been found to give evidence in support of Dunn's accusations
of high treason, so this charge had been dropped, and replaced
by one accusing ten of the societies' members of conspiring to
overthrow the King, Constitution and Government, and "to
aid and assist the French in case of invasion".

\*          \*          \*

The trial took place at Lancaster in the Spring Assizes, on
2nd April, 1794. Eight of the ten accused were in the court,
MacCallum and Smith having left for America; beside Walker
and Samuel Jackson in the dock, were Booth, Paul, Cheetham,
Pearsall (all described as "labourers"), Henry York ("gentleman") and Dr. Joseph Collier the surgeon.

Mr. Law, who had formerly so ably prosecuted Walker's
enemy Roberts, had come back to prosecute Walker. He found
himself confronted by an impressive party for the defence, led,
as we have mentioned, by Thomas Erskine, and including Felix
Vaughan and Thomas Lloyd. Mr. Justice Heath presided; it

[1] Walker Trial.

would have been hard to find a more biassed judge, but this did not unduly worry Erskine, who habitually pinned his faith to the justness of his cause and the fairness of the jury.

The indictment, when it was read out, must have sounded quite fantastic to the prisoners and their friends—and indeed to anyone in that court not completely blinded by political prejudice; of the eight accused, it was said, among other things, that they were "wicked, seditious and ill-disposed persons" intending "as much as in them lay to break the peace and disturb the tranquillity of this kingdom", and "to aid and assist the French . . . in case such enemies should enter into and invade this kingdom in a warlike and hostile manner"; of Walker, it was said that he was "pernicious" as well as seditious and ill-disposed. And that he had been heard "maliciously and seditiously to utter publish and declare the words . . . 'What are Kings damn the King (meaning our said Lord the now King) what is he (meaning our said Lord the King) to us if I (meaning the said Thomas Walker) had him (meaning our said Lord the King) in my power I (meaning etc. etc.) would as soon take his (meaning etc. etc.) head off as I (meaning etc. etc.) would tear this paper,' he the said Thomas Walker then and there tearing in pieces a piece of paper which he then and there had and held in his hand to the great scandal of our said Lord the King and his Laws . . .".

An extra indictment against Cheetham was that he was reported (by Dunn) to have said: "I wish he (meaning our said Lord the King) was in New Bailey Prison instead of Benjamin Booth."

Law did his level best to advance a presentable case; but the slenderness of his chances of success were obvious, when he spoke at length about the attack that Erskine would be sure to make on Dunn's character: "The evidence of this person [Dunn] will unquestionably be assailed and attacked and his character arraigned . . ." and warned the audience against being swayed by this. Of Erskine he said: "I know the ingenious sophistry [of my learned friend] by which he can mislead, and the fascination of that eloquence by which he can subdue the minds of those to whom he addresses himself."

Even had Erskine been given to "ingenious sophistry"

(which, whatever Mr. Law might suggest, he most certainly was not) there was no need of any, in this case. It was clear from the moment Dunn appeared in the witness box that there was something very peculiar indeed about his evidence; to begin with, when asked what the "intent" of the Constitutional Society was, he answered thus: "I absolutely will just inform you candidly in my opinion as far as I can learn when I came to understand myself properly that it was to overthrow the whole constitution."

The methods adopted by the society to this end, according to him, were the reading of Paine's works, and listening to revolutionary speakers in Walker's house, while drilling went on in the warehouse at the back, with muskets and bayonets. Dunn remarked that when he went to Walker's home for the first time, the merchant had met him on the stairs, and perceiving he was from Ireland, asked him "how the Volunteers were going on?" On hearing Dunn's reply, "Very prosperous", he "just waved his hand and said 'We would overthrow the constitution by and by.' " The Irishman said that Yorke, a well-known democrat, had come over from Sheffield to see what could be done to assist the French if they should land.—"Fifty thousand French were expected." Jackson, Dunn said, "recommended everything to be very candid and keep every thing very secret, that we should be unanimous one to another . . ."

In the course of cross-examination, the other witness, Kinnaston the constable, described how he watched Walker's house all through January and February, between 6 and 9 at night, once or twice a week; he leaned against the wall nearby, and watched the members of the societies being let in after giving "a very gentle tap".

When asked how he could hear the very gentle tap, being well known to be rather hard of hearing, Mr. Kinnaston replied: "I was not deaf then."

Erskine's speech for the defence was a magnificent peroration. He began by putting to the jury how very serious the charge was "that had been thus brought against a merchant of honour, property, character and respect; who has long enjoyed the friendship of many of the worthiest and most illustrious persons in the kingdom, and whose principles and conduct have more than once been publicly acknowledged by the community".

Speaking of the time when the societies had been turned out of the public houses (after the publicans, "probably directed by the magistrates, thought fit to shut up their houses, opened by immemorial law to all the King's subjects, and to refuse admission to all the gentlemen and tradesmen of the town who did not associate under the banners of this Church and King club"), Erskine asked: "Could it be attributed to Mr. Walker as seditious that he honourably stood forth and opened his house to a society of Gentlemen and Tradesmen whose good principles he was acquainted with?" As to the Society's right to entertain opinions other than Tory ones: "In all public measures the decision is undoubtedly with government, but the people have a right to think upon them and express what they think."

Referring to Walker and his friends' campaign for peace, Erskine went on: "Surely *War* of all other subjects is one which the people have the right to consider; surely it can be no offence for those whose properties were to be taxed and whose inheritance were to be lessened by it, to pause a little upon the eve of a contest the end of which no man can calculate, nor estimate the blood to flow from its calamities? Surely it is a liberty secured to us by the first principles of our constitution, to address the sovereign or instruct our representatives to avert the greatest evil that can impend over a nation?"

Dunn's remarks about meeting Walker on the staircase, drew forth Erskine's most scathing comments: "Gentlemen," he said, "would you pull a feather out of a sparrow's wing upon the oath of a man who swears a person to have been a good subject, in the very moment he was telling him of an intended rebellion? Could any man but a driveller have possibly given such an answer as is put into Mr. Walker's mouth to a man he had never seen in his life? However many may differ from Mr. Walker in opinion, everybody, I believe, will admit that he is an acute intelligent man, with an extensive knowledge of the world, and not at all likely to have conducted himself like an idiot."

He went on to ask what interest Walker could possibly have

L

in forwarding a French invasion, and he suggests that the merchant had on the contrary a great deal to lose. "His friends, some of the best men in this kingdom would be destroyed if this invasion took place." His family life would be grievously affected. Here Erskine mentioned that Thomas "is the husband of an amiable and affectionate woman, and the happy parent of six engaging children".

"Could we look at this moment into the dwelling of this unfortunate gentleman," he said, "I am persuaded it would distress us; they cannot but be unhappy: they have seen prosecutions equally unjust as even this is, attended with a success of equal injustice, and we have seen those proceedings by those who are at the bottom of this indictment, put forward for your imitation."

Erskine then talked about the peaceful nature of the Constitutional Society, and of the desirability of parliamentary reform, and quoted some of the current abuses of the electoral system. He concluded by saying that "unjust prosecutions lead to the ruin of all governments", and he hoped that the Attorney-General would feel "that a prosecution like this ought not to be offered for the seal and sanction of your [the jury's] verdict".

He then proceeded to call his witnesses. One after another declared that the meetings of the societies were quiet and orderly, that the literature was respectable reformist matter, that the speakers were informative and sedate; the picture given suggested a serious-minded study group, rather than a body of revolutionaries fomenting anarchy and confusion.

Nobody had ever heard Walker damn the King, or anything similar; nobody had ever heard Paine's *Rights of Man* read out; nobody had ever seen any sign of "manual exercise". The only guns that any witnesses had ever noticed were those collected during and after the December riots, for self-defence—a few old muskets and blunderbusses, later locked away.

Erskine gave a delightful description of the collection of weapons: "Last week," he said, "I was shown into this house of conspiracy, treason and death, and saw exposed to view the mighty armoury which was to level the beautiful fabrick of our constitution and to destroy the lives and properties of seven millions of people." He described the six little swivel guns ("so-called because they turn upon a pivot"), "in this case taken off their props, painted, and put upon blocks; in that shape they may fairly be called children's toys. You frequently see them in the neighbourhood of London, adorning the houses of sober citizens, who, preferring grandeur to taste, place them upon their ramparts at Mile End or Islington."

Erskine said these "swivels" had been fired only twice: on the Prince of Wales' birthday, and "on the occasion of his Majesty's happy recovery" (and we know of another time—the night of the repeal of the Fustian Tax); "these are the only times these cannon big with destruction had opened their little mouths".

He told the court how he went "under the protection of the master-general of this ordnance, Mr. Walker's Chambermaid, to visit the rest of this formidable array of death, and found next a little musketoon about so high. I put my thumb upon it, when out started a little bayonet like the Jack-in-a-Box we buy for children at a fair. Apart from this there lay three or four rusty guns, and here and there a bayonet or broadsword covered over with dust or dirt."

Even had there been more arms about, the witnesses all denied ever having seen them in use. The servants, Mary Denham, Martha Wilkinson and Francis Roberts, had never seen nor heard any sign of drilling. The question was put, "if any noise, for instance the clatter of ramrods . . . had happened, you could have heard them?" and was answered in the affirmative.

Martha, "though not constantly watching", declared she would certainly have known if anything of the sort had been going on, and the other witnesses concurred.

Mr. Duckworth, Walker's solicitor, moreover, gave the height of the warehouse room, where it was alleged that arms practice took place, as eight feet six inches under the highest beams, seven and a half feet under the lowest. "I took a musket and fixed the bayonet to shoulder it," he said. "When I shouldered it the point of the bayonet touched the ceiling; if I had thrown it up to my shoulder the bayonet would have stuck in the ceiling." This alone should have been conclusive enough to dispose of the charge of training an infantry battalion to aid and assist the French!

Some evidence was given to show that Dunn tried to avoid appearing in court, and this was distorted by the counsel for the Crown to seem as though Walker had wished it so, and attempted to get Dunn out of the way. But it was proved that, on the contrary, Walker had sent an employee to Liverpool and to Preston to fetch the Irishman back, and to make sure, by subpoenaing him, that he would be present at the assizes.

Finally, Mr. Seddon described Dunn's visit to Walker on 18th March, of which he had taken verbatim notes. Dunn was called back into court for examination about this, and he came rolling in, completely drunk. When the judge asked him whether he remembered the events described by Mr. Seddon— "Did that pass, or any part of it?"—he replied: "No, nothing at all—yes, something of it passed. . . . I went there when I was intoxicated, the same as I am now. . . ."

After some very incoherent answers, the Judge broke in; "I don't know how we can examine a man that is drunk."

Law tried in vain to get some sense out of his key witness: "Did you beg Mr. Walker to sit along side of you, and say you would esteem it as great an honour as if George III did?"—"I never said that, upon my oath," was Dunn's retort.

Mr. Justice Heath intervened again: "How can you, Mr. Law, examine him? . . . He has made himself so exceedingly drunk it is impossible to examine him." However the cross-questioning went on, until Mr. Thomas Jones, an unquestionably reputable local lawyer, gave an account from his notes of the scene of Dunn's confession to Walker, as witnessed by himself and the two other gentlemen. Dunn flatly denied every word of this.

Erskine asked him: "Mr. Thomas Dunn, is this true or false?"

"False," replied Dunn. "This gentleman is perjured then— it is all false?"—"Yes," said Dunn.

At this, Mr. Law, with the air of one about to make a supreme sacrifice, stood up. "I know the character of several of the gentlemen," he said. "Particularly Mr. Jones. I cannot expect one witness alone, unconfirmed, to stand against the testimony of these witnesses; I ought not to expect it."

The judge remarked: "You act very properly, Mr. Law."

The jury, without even leaving the room, immediately gave their verdict, NOT GUILTY. On which Felix Vaughan jumped to his feet, saying, "I pray Dunn may be committed." Erskine added, "We will undertake to prosecute him for Perjury."

Mr. Justice Heath nodded: "Let him be committed." Then, turning to Walker he added, "And I hope, Mr. Walker, this will be an admonition to you to keep better company in future."

Thomas answered, with considerable indignation: "I have been in no bad company, my Lord, except in that of the wretch who stands behind me; nor is there a word or an action in my life, in which the public are at all interested, that I wish unsaid, or undone, or that under similar circumstances I would not repeat."

The tragic farce was not quite ended: the jury had to be re-impannelled for the acquittal of Thomas Walker on the second charge (of tearing the King's Head); and yet again, for the acquittal of James Cheetham on the charge of wishing to guillotine the King. And yet once more, to commit Dunn for perjury.[1]

Although at the end of the afternoon Walker left the court with his head high, "honourably acquitted", he was three thousand pounds the poorer, owing to the expenses involved in the defence of the case. And although he had no stain on his character, the slander and smear campaign of the previous ten months had damaged his health, and done great harm to his business . . . how great, no one could foresee. He had learned some of the unpleasant facts of life under the Pitt régime—but at an exorbitant cost.

[1] Walker Trial.

## CHAPTER XVI

## COUNTING THE COST (1794 and after)

WALKER'S acquittal was hailed by his friends as a victory for truth as well as a personal triumph. Six days after the trial, Fox wrote to him assuring him "that I have seldom felt more true satisfaction than I received from Heywood's letter from Lancaster, giving me the account of your complete triumph there. Your satisfaction ought to be (and I hope is) proportionate to the malignancy with which you have been persecuted; and if it is, you must be a very happy man. I beg you accept my sincere congratulations, and to believe me, dear Sir, your most faithful, humble servant, C. J. Fox."

Addressing him as "Dear Citizen", Lord Stanhope wrote: "I beg to congratulate you most cordially and sincerely on your late acquittal; as also the other gentlemen indicted at the same time; being with zeal and respect, Sir, your faithful fellow-citizen, Stanhope." There is a comment on the margin of this note to the effect that "many years afterwards this republican peer had his portrait taken with a coronet in his hand! such is the influence of circumstances".

Gilbert Wakefield, the distinguished classical scholar, in a letter of 17th July, congratulated Thomas on "the defeat of his despicable adversaries", and was sure he would rejoice with Wakefield "on the glorious prospect of a speedy crisis to the abominable perversions of civil society . . ." Clarkson, the mainspring of the great anti-slavery campaign, was overjoyed at the acquittal; he mentioned, in his letter of congratulation, that Lord Derby had been violently abusive to the Ministry about the trial "and reprobated the conduct of the prosecutors severely".

It seems that the trial caused a sensation in London; on 26th April Thomas Erskine wrote pressing Walker to let him have proofs of the shorthand notes: "I take for granted you will publish it in Manchester, and I am sure it will be of infinite service to the cause of reform and bring the Government into great disgrace."

A month later another letter from Erskine said: "Your friends here are much disappointed at not seeing your trial published, and there are catchpenny things circulated to pass for it. It certainly throws great light upon the businesses which agitate the public at this moment, and its appearance now would be useful."[1]

However delighted his friends may have been, Walker himself felt very little satisfaction. He had suffered too much in the process which could never be compensated. Justice had prevailed, but at what cost! The trial of Dunn (for which Walker had to pay) was no cause for rejoicing: the Irishman, tried "upon an indictment containing no less than ten several perjuries, which he had sworn against Walker and the others . . ." was found guilty, "and the sentence of Mr. Justice Rooke was, that he should stand once in the pillory and be imprisoned for two years in Lancaster Castle".[2]

This was small comfort to Thomas; he knew that Dunn was a miserable creature, who, under the influence of drink, had said what he was bribed or bullied into saying; the sentence should have been passed on the instigators of the whole iniquitous business, and they should have been forced to make compensation to the sufferers. They should at the very least have revealed who bore the initial costs. As Thomas said, it was naturally asked "by what means the prosecutor Dunn, who was not worth one farthing, should be able to bear the expence of an unsuccessful prosecution, of which the pecuniary burthen fell so heavy on the defendants who were acquitted?"

"I do not know," he goes on, "who paid Messrs. Milne and Sergeant, the Manchester agents for the prosecution, nor can I yet tell at whose command, and at whose charge Mr. Shelton first came down from London. If individuals have taken all this trouble, borne this heavy expence, it is singular they should remain unknown. . . . If the public have defrayed this expence, if the Officers of Government have it in their power to apply the purse of the nation to institute suits against individuals whose opposition to public abuses may render them obnoxious,

[1] Jerrold, p. 73.                    [2] Walker, *Review*, p. 89.

there is an end of the liberty of speech, the liberty of the press, and the liberty of the subject."

Walker then shows that he is well aware that the prosecution was directed from London: "There is no standing against the forms and fictions of the law when put in motion by the purse of the Treasury. Of what consequence is it, whether a man be imprisoned in a jail for life because he cannot pay a thousand pounds, at the expence of a law-suit, or a thousand pounds as a fine? How many innocent and worthy men are there, whom the defence of the accusations against us would have compleatly ruined! Gold may be bought too dear, and so may justice. I should be glad to obtain it but I cannot afford it."

He goes on to explain that, if he could, he would have prosecuted some of those "who expected and perhaps wished that I should be overwhelmed by the prosecution", and had made "insidious though unsuspected attacks upon my character and credit as a merchant, both at home and abroad. . . . But were I to pursue the offenders by legal means, my whole life would be spent in litigation. . . ."

Elsewhere, he says "without scruple", and "from dear-bought experience, that there is no law in this country for the poor man. The expence of attorneys, and the expence of counsel, and the expence of witnesses, and the expence of Stamps to the Government, and fees to the Law Officers, the expence of time, and of trouble, the neglect of business and the anxiety of mind, are beyond calculation to those who have not had melancholy experience of the fact." Neither, says he, gloomily, is there any certainty of justice "even to those who are able and willing to afford the expence of a prosecution, if the minds of the Jurors can be warped on the day of trial from all impartial considerations, by incessant falsehood and invective, from pulpits and printing-houses and parish associations".

"I have a right to complain of the uncertainty of justice, after the trial of Benjamin Booth at Manchester; after having perused the trials of Mr. Winterbotham; after having seen the verdicts of a Warwickshire jury, and compared the compensations with the losses of the Birmingham sufferers."

As to Windham's remark in the House of Commons, that "the law was equally open in all cases", Thomas says "it was a cruel and malignant sarcasm . . . and Mr. Windham could not but know that it was untrue when he uttered it. The law is indeed open to those who have the key of the Treasury to unlock it—it was open even to Thomas Dunn of infamous notoriety. Perhaps it would be open also to Mr. Windham—from the tender mercies of whose recommendation in this instance, heaven defend the injured poor!"[1]

The cost of litigation for the defendants in State trials was indeed a very burning question during the year 1794. All over the country men were being prosecuted for "seditious practices" of one sort and another. One might have thought that Walker's trial—a completely catastrophic example of organised injustice, exposing the organisers to general ridicule and shame—would have been a warning, in Erskine's words, "that unjust prosecutions lead to the ruin of all governments"; but it seems that this government was willing to court ruin if it could thereby have the blood of a few men of differing political opinions.

A series of prosecutions took place, beginning with William Frend, a scholar of Cambridge, who had written an anti-war pamphlet (quoted earlier), and William Winterbotham, a dissenting minister, sentenced to four years imprisonment, after two trials, for a sermon with a questionable text.

The men most wanted by the Ministry were, of course, the leaders of the popular societies, and particularly of the London Corresponding Society, who were fearlessly carrying on their activity in spite of the repression; collections were being made for the "Scottish martyrs" before their prison ships sailed for Australia; at meetings and dinners, the toasts were "Three times three" for Margarot, and "May Botany Bay be peopled with *real* criminals". The divisions of the L.C.S. continued their work, and a mass meeting was organised on 14th April at Chalk Farm, to protest at the war, and to congratulate Stanhope on his motion in the House of Lords against interference in France.

A resolution was unanimously passed at this meeting, showing the general preoccupation with police methods: "That any attempt to violate those yet remaining laws, which were intended for the security of Englishmen against the Tyranny of

---

[1] Walker, *Review*, pp. 89-90.

M

Courts and Ministers, and the Corruption of dependent Judges, ought to be considered as dissolving entirely the social Compact between the English Nation and their Governors."

According to an informer, Thelwall made jokes about the spies present, one of them named Lavender; and he told them they might inform Government that they had had "an opportunity of learning good manners, order, and decorum from the Swinish Multitude".[1]

This defiance thoroughly riled the government, who were waiting for any pretext to pounce. They found one on the occasion of the dinner party given by the Constitutional Society (to which L.C.S. members were admitted free) on 2nd May, and at which the toasts were reported (by the government's agents) to be highly seditious.

On 12th May they swooped: Thomas Hardy, the L.C.S. secretary, was arrested and all his papers seized. On 15th May, a Secret Committee was formed in the House of Commons, and on the strength of a report compiled by this committee (which included Pitt, Dundas and Windham) Parliament was asked for, and accorded, a special Act to suspend Habeas Corpus. This was to enable the government to hold suspects in custody without further evidence.

Within a week most of the leaders of the Corresponding Society were arrested and taken to the Tower or to Newgate. Some members of the Constitutional Society were also taken, including Daniel Adams the secretary. It is sad to relate that this stalwart bought his freedom by giving information about the society, and was never brought to trial. The "Constitutionals" as a whole were not remarkable for their courage; in fact, they were only a degree less cautious than the "Friends of the People" (that club of the élite, to which Sheridan, Grey and other Whig Members of Parliament belonged), who had refused any sort of co-operation with more Radical groups, and had closed down their organisation in 1793 when things were getting difficult.

The L.C.S. members were far braver in standing up to the merciless persecution, and there was praiseworthy solidarity with those in gaol. One spy's report mentions that "it was

[1] Privy Council Papers, A.35, 1794.

recommended to the members of this division to encourage Hardy [the shoe-maker secretary, now in gaol] by each having a pair of shoes of him, and to circulate his cards through all the Divisions and recommend the same". Indignation was reported by the same spy, at "the apprehension of Hardy and Adams", which was "said to be an artful manœuvre to make Parliament swallow a Convention Bill, and that the Societies instead of being intimidated ought to be more strongly united".[1]

Felix Vaughan and Thomas Lloyd and others helped to carry on the organisation in the absence of the nine or ten leading spirits who were kept in prison all through the summer, under conditions of extreme discomfort. Many applications were made to the Privy Council by their wives and friends, for permission to alleviate their hardships. Thelwall's wife asked for him to be allowed writing materials; others asked for books and newspapers; others for more visitors; Horne Tooke— although he wrote that "the police had behaved perfectly well, and if he was a Traitor he had been used too well, but if not, too ill"—suffered from dropsy, and asked, through Vaughan, to be allowed to sleep alone.

He also wrote personally, asking for his own doctor to visit him—"as my private affairs have been laid open to the Privy Council, I feel no great repugnance to lay open to them my more private bodily infirmities, which their warrant now reaches by consequence".[2]

There was no doubt that the Ministers were uneasy about their action in imprisoning these well-known and popular figures, and about the possible result of the trial—which was of course disastrous for them, all their victims being victoriously acquitted.

Dundas betrayed some of his anxiety in a letter of 26th October, 1794, in which he says, "I have this day signed a Writ for a warrant against Callender. But I think unless his conduct is very atrocious it should not be put into Execution till the London Trials are over. . . . I sincerely hope by the time you receive this that the trial at least of Hardy, is well over."[3]

Spies and informers everywhere were quaking at the thought

[1] Privy Council Papers, A.35, 1794.    [2] Ibid.    [3] Ibid.

of their unpopularity and its effects on their livelihood: as Mr. Reeves said in his report, "the persons who give information could not be brought forward for fear of their lives".[1]

One of them writes, on 2nd June, "I rely on your word given, that I am not to be brought forward on the Trials of these men. I have suffered much in this business for my loyalty to my King and Country, and am likely to suffer more. If I was brought forward against these men it would be my ruin." Others complained of offensive or threatening notices being stuck on their doors.[2]

All of which shows that there was considerable latent public indignation against the methods used to damage the democrats, and that a firm stand by the Whigs would have found a mass backing, and might well have secured the freedom of the prisoners, and the retreat of the government.

However, very few were valorous enough to risk championing the persecuted Radicals in the face of authority. To come back to Thomas Walker's case, there could have been nothing to lose by supporting a man of such position and prestige, but the so-called "friends of the people" failed to stand by him. As Walker said: "there are indeed some individuals whose generous and decided conduct on the occasion of this trial has made an impression on my mind which will never be erased; but the general treatment I have experienced has been such as I have stated"—numerous cases of "insidious and systematic attacks" on him. Walker commented on the attitude of his "friends" and of his enemies with great bitterness, and at considerable length. His conclusions carry such a general and ageless ring, that some extracts of what he wrote are worth quoting:

"My own experience has convinced me," he said, "firstly, that of all the corporations (the privileged orders) of this kingdom, the clergy are the most sore upon the subject of reformation. . . . Next to the Clergy (very many of whom are also Justices) the Justices of the Peace (nominated by the influence of the Crown) have been the most active against political discussion and reformation, and the most prominent and obsequious agents of ministerial alarm."

Secondly, "that there is little or no dependence to be placed

---

[1] Treasury Solicitor's Papers, 3495.    [2] Ibid.

upon those who zealously mix religious with political questions, or *who only from sectarian motives join in political societies.* The Dissenters . . . have as a body constantly fallen short of their own principles—through fear or some other motive *they have been so strongly the advocates of an Overstrained Moderation, that they have rather been the enemies than the friends of those who have ventured the most and effected the most for the rights of the people.*"

Next, "that almost all the attacks upon individuals, which their enemies have directly or indirectly ventured upon—and which have in the background so many men of good intentions, but whom an excess of caution, or a timid kind of prudence has prevented from acting—have been owing to a want of steadiness and concert among the friends of Liberty themselves. The timid desert the bold, till the bold become cautious of supporting each other with their presence and unable to do so with their property."

"Neither the Birmingham riots, nor the Manchester riots, nor the prosecutions, public or private which have taken place, would have happened, had not the timidity and want of union amongst the friends of freedom emboldened their enemies.

"Temper and moderation are truly valuable; but the professionally temperate men have been the first deserters from, and have uniformly done infinite mischief to, the rights of the people."

Walker adds, rather pathetically: "Men who mean to do good, must not look for their reward, or the effect of their exertions, during the existing generation. Such an effect they may indeed live to see, but it cannot be counted upon. Those who are not capable of acting upon this hazard, are not the men upon whom the public can fully depend; or who can pursue a great plan of public utility with satisfaction to themselves."

He himself was, we know, capable of "acting upon this hazard". He was temporarily disillusioned just after the trial, and for a short time decided to drop politics—James Watt tells his father (September, 1794) that "I believe our friends have done with politics forever, and that they will now devote those abilities to the prosecution of their own business, which have hitherto been employed for the good of others"; but Thomas Cooper's less elegantly-worded remark, in April, 1794, rings truer: "Walker I fancy is determined to stay in this country as long as he can. I fear he is irrevocably bitten with the politico mania. . . ."

The truth was, that he felt that it was only through political action that anything of social importance or for the public good could be achieved; and so he very soon resumed his interest in things, and continued to "act upon hazard". He lived twenty-two years longer, and thus saw some slight "effect of his exertions" in the public field—all too slight, unfortunately. However, he never doubted that "when the day of reformation shall come, as come it must", things would be different. One can only regret that he did not live to see many of his own great plans of public utility bearing fruit, in the shape of future reforms and measures of social welfare, particularly, perhaps, free and universal education. For he strongly condemned "the want of a compleat and universal system of public education" which "rendered the mass of the people . . . so generally adverse to their friends, and so blindly the dupes of their oppressors".

The last words of his *Review*, written with the deepest conviction, are that "Ignorance—public Ignorance, is the sole cause of Political Evil and the great Bane of Human Happiness."[1]

[1] Walker, *Review*, pp. 123-7.

## CHAPTER XVII

# AFTERMATH

THE purpose of this sketch of Thomas Walker and his circle was to throw a spotlight on their lives and doings during those few years alone. But perhaps, as the light fades out on the good and the bad, the honest and the unscrupulous, the attractive and the repulsive characters of the brief drama, we may be allowed to follow them till they are engulfed in the darkness of time.

We catch a flickering glimpse of several of them in the later years of their lives, in the notes recorded by a scratchy pen in an interleaved *Directory of Manchester* for 1794.

Here, for instance, we learn that several of the "Church and King" club gentlemen made fortunes—while the democrats usually failed in their businesses.

Some of the Tory gentlemen, however, came to a sticky end. Of the notorious Reverend Maurice Griffith, for instance, we read the comment: "He was a magistrate as was his son, but their conduct being disapproved of, they were struck off of the commission." Nathaniel Milne, the magistrate who so conscientiously looked out for libellous literature, died "of gout in his stomach, in 1809". Nathan Crompton, chairman of one of the Manchester Associations, "died in 1800—his son proved to be a great villian". Of Richard Paynter, one of Benjamin Booth's inquisitors, we read: "His wife's sister had a child by him; after which he sunk into disgrace, drank, and died."

Richard Unite "went to the Isle of Man with an indifferent character"—and we know from another source that he was turned out of his post as overseer to the poor, for disgraceful practices of one sort and another. Thomas Kinnaston, Salford Constable and witness against Walker, was "removed from his office—he was disgraced and died a pauper".

As for Thomas Dunn, his death is recorded in the July 1798 *Monthly Magazine*, as occurring "at Manchester, in extreme wretchedness, unpitied and detested by mankind". A telling comment on the fate of those who allow themselves to be bribed or bought by their "betters".

Two sad figures in this shadowy procession are Twiss, Walker's employee (he appeared briefly during the trial) who "drowned himself in his own fishpond in April, 1803"; and Benjamin Booth—dogged by misfortune to the very last—whose wife "died suddenly when making preparation for company". Two years later, "having company himself one day he arose, went to the window and said what pain I have at my breast; dropped down and died".

Of the other Radicals, the records are nearly all sad: Collier, the gifted surgeon, "left the town in 1804, went to Sheffield and in 1806 was confined in the Lunatic Asylum in York". Samuel Jackson, one-time secretary of the Constitutional Society, failed in business and became an "accomptant", dying in 1817.

Dr. Ferriar, of the Infirmary, distinguished and respected as he was, died insolvent, in 1815. Matthew Falkner, the progressive printer, "failed"; "he went to America, but returned later, and died at Burnley, aged 86". The commentator adds that Falkner "ruined himself by joining the leaders of the Constitutional Society; he was a quiet inoffensive man, and the tool of the Democrats, Cooper, the Walkers and Samuel Jackson, the black Cat".

Thomas Cooper was more fortunate than most; he escaped before he could be ruined, in spite of appeals from Felix Vaughan to stay. "If *good men* would not leave us," wrote Vaughan, "what might we not attempt for the good people of England! as to the bad, it signifies little what becomes of them. In sober sadness cast in your mind whether you cannot bear with us for a few years more and help us to stem the torrent of folly. . . ."

But Cooper went. He settled with Dr. Joseph Priestley in Sunbury, Pennyslvania, where he started and edited a Radical newspaper, the *Republican Weekly Advertiser*. In a letter from America written on 29th September, 1795 he tells Walker that "Dr. Priestley continues writing on Religion, and people smile. His wife is very ill"—while Cooper himself is "in high favour with the People here". (Undue modesty was never a characteristic of Cooper's, and the United States had not changed him.) "If the endeavours prove successful you may perhaps have to direct your letters by and by to the Hon. Judge Cooper"; he is however cautious enough to add: "However, as that is not quite settled as yet, the less said about it the better."

Poor Cooper! he was to be sadly disillusioned in his ideas of the brave new world to which he had escaped: getting into trouble with the administration of President John Adams, through the Alien and Sedition Act of 1798, he was sentenced in 1800 to six months imprisonment and a fine of four hundred dollars for a libel upon the President. The English refugees were so little appreciated that Adams was reported as exclaiming: "Just Heavens! . . . to what are we coming when our laws, our government, or sovereignty, are thus usurped and trampled under the feet of wandering vagabonds?" The President also said that Priestley was "weak as water", and "not an Atom in the World".—"Tom Cooper was the villain of the piece, and had led Priestley into mischief".

However Cooper received some compensation later, and confirmation of his earlier hopes, when the Republicans returned to office, and he was appointed a High Commissioner, and later, presiding judge of the Pennsylvania Court of Common Pleas. Removed on a charge of arbitrary conduct in 1811, he was made professor of mineralogy and chemistry in Pennsylvania University in 1819, and eventually became president of South Carolina College, Columbia. We are told by Leary, the Manchester journalist, that President Adams referred to him as "that learned, ingenuous, scientific and talented madcap", intending, possibly, by these semi-complimentary words to make up for previous insults.

To return to Manchester and to the Walkers: we find them down in the 1794 *Directory* as "Walker, Thomas and Richard, merchants and fustian-manufacturers, back of 7 South-parade", with a note by the owner of the book—"failed". He adds a brief outline of their later lives: Richard, we learn, "went to France and was confined many weeks in the Temple at Paris. On being liberated he went into Italy to collect debts for their creditor, who allowed his family £300 during his absence. In 1808 Richard went to Sicily . . . he has never returned to England." We are left to wonder what became of Mrs. W.,

Harriet, and the "fine boy" who was James Watt's godson, and to hope that Richard provided for them while he was in Sicily!

Thomas, the note says, "lives at Longford. Several friends made a handsome subscription for him in 1801."

But it is the word "failed" that sticks in the memory. Thomas's enemies had their victory and their revenge after all, for there is no reason to suppose that the Walker firm would not have weathered the storm if destruction of their credit, and ruin through the huge expenses of the trial, had not been deliberately organised.

Business failure was almost as severe a penalty as imprisonment for Thomas, who had written: "in this Country if a Man possesses every Virtue under Heaven, and wants a Guinea, he can do little good, either to himself or others".[1]

The witch-hunters had succeeded in breaking his business, and in the process his health and—almost—his spirit. The strain, the struggle to survive, the humiliations he had suffered, all told on him, and are reflected in some of his letters; several mention illness: "I have been attacked by a very violent inflammation with a very considerable degree of Fever"—"Mrs. W.'s health is very indifferent and my own will not bear any close confinement" (1800); others reveal great unhappiness: ". . . my situation would be insupportable was it imbittered by the reflexions that it had been brought on by any meanness, any extravagance or any crime of my own . . ."; and much anxiety about his children: "As no man has a greater affection for his family than I have, so no man could make greater exertions to promote their welfare than I would; but hitherto all my endeavours have been ineffectual, nor has anything yet been proposed to me that would mend my present situation, uncomfortable as it is, but rather the reverse . . ." and "for the education of my Boys I am very anxious. Education, you will allow, is a foundation without which no superstructure of any consequence, can reasonably be expected to be raised. I have no ambitions to see my children what the world calls great; but I am extremely solicitous that they should be honest and wise."

He was very keen that his eldest boy, Thomas, should go to Cambridge University, and writing to James Watt junior in

[1] Walker-Watt Correspondence.

1803 confesses that "I wish him to have every advantage which it is possible to derive from education . . . and form an intimate connexion with those whose friendship every honourable man would wish to cultivate". He says that he would much like young Thomas to meet James's father, the inventor. "Was I entering into life, highly as property is to be estimated, I would much rather possess his knowledge than his fortune."

Other worries beset Walker at this time: "My eldest daughter is not so well . . . she may linger for some months, but of her recovery I am *very* doubtful. Margaret my second daughter is likewise very seriously indisposed. The rest of my family are as well, as under such circumstances can reasonably be expected."[1]

We know from letters such as these that Walker suffered very deeply from his troubles. Nevertheless he refused to be crushed by them, and thanks to his natural resilience he managed to keep up his interest in public affairs and even take an active part in them. From the small farm at Longford (four miles from the centre of Manchester, to which he moved before the turn of the century), he corresponded with his friends, and sent them garden produce. In 1798 he was dispatching "some Nectarine stones and Strawberry seeds" to Thomas Cooper in Pennsylvania; and sending apricots and Lancashire apples and pears to Charles James Fox, along with letters on the subject of the Slave Trade and the East India Company's Monopoly.

Letters of thanks for presents of this sort and many others abounded in his correspondence; Erskine wrote that "the gift [of some of Thomas' muslins] will be valued not merely for the beauty of the manufacture, but for the respect I have for the giver".

From Horne Tooke came the assurance, on 10th February, 1796, that "your gooseberries and potatoes shall be carefully planted, and I will not spare manure. Justice shall be done to them, and the same I promise to any other things or persons which you may at any time put into my hands. Justice to Red Traitors!"

The picture which this letter evokes of Horne Tooke planting the fruit and vegetables, is confirmed by a letter from Felix Vaughan to Thomas Cooper in America (28th January, 1796):

[1] Walker-Watt Correspondence.

"Tooke digs in his garden till he is out of breath, by which he has certainly increased his health so as to live many years longer; at least I hope so. . . ." He adds: "None of us are very rich, and some very poor, democracy being, as you well know, one of Pharaoh's lean kine."

Vaughan says he considers himself "as the most thriving, although perhaps I am not the least obnoxious, of those who profess public principles. The lawyers . . . being for some reason or other more formidable in the eyes of Government than other people. I can give no other reason for having escaped their vengeance. In the way of my profession I have been very successful, both in Yorkshire and Lancashire; for the latter I need not say I am indebted to you and Walker."[1]

Walker's correspondence throws what dim light there is on his later life. It is clear, from replies of Erskine and Fox, that he had written asking for their help in getting some civil service post, such as Commissioner of Customs in the Port of London, for which he would have been well fitted. But they seem to have lacked either the power or the will to help him, for he never obtained such a position. He found even less of a spirit of helpfulness in his nearer neighbours. Writing in 1804 to Major John Cartwright, the eminent fighter for reform, Walker remarked that he had recently been in Manchester, "where I have seen several persons who profess themselves the friends of freedom and of Sir Francis Burdett; but I am very sorry to say that neither their love of the former, nor their respect for the latter, will lead them to make any effort in support of their professions.

"Apathy and timidity seem at present, to be the order of the day in a place which some years ago did not confine itself to *wishing*. . . . A wicked and a corrupt Minister is a much more dangerous enemy than any foreign one; but a money-mongering and a besotted people are worse than either. . . ."

Thomas did not, however, let either apathy or timidity dismay him for long; as we have already said, he seems, in spite of everything, to have taken an active and prominent part in public life for a great many years. In 1808 he was deeply engaged in a Manchester Waterworks Bill; in June, 1813 he was

[1] Jerrold, p. 110.

pleading the cause of his home town and describing its dreadful condition to Lord Dundas, while advising him how to act in the matter; in 1812 he was subscribing to the fund for the defence of "Mr. Knight and the 36 other friends of Peace and Reform", then imprisoned in Lancaster Castle, and getting Lord Brougham (through his friend Major Cartwright) to take up their case.[1]

His generosity was not warped by the losses he suffered through the trial, but he would have been in real want had he not been helped by some staunch friends; the best of these was Felix Vaughan, who, as a last gesture of solidarity, left him most of his money; thanks to this, Walker was able to live his last years in comparative comfort, and leave his family provided for. His wife survived him, and his sons appear to have looked after her, while themselves doing well in various professional fields. Charles became a magistrate who "enjoyed a high reputation for his public spirit" and "his devotion to the public weal in Lancashire";[2] the eldest boy, Thomas, is known by readers of nineteenth-century curiosities as the author of the *Original*, a weekly magazine appearing from May, 1835 onwards; he was educated at Trinity College, Cambridge, and became a barrister, and a would-be reformer of the Poor Laws, which he constantly and violently attacked in his journal.

\*         \*         \*

The last glimpse we get of Walker is given by William Godwin, in a letter written on 30th April, 1816, where he describes a visit to "Thomas Walker, the famous republican of the times of Gerrald, whom I had encountered two or three times at the house of Horne Tooke, about twenty years ago. . . .

"The venerable old gentleman lives at Longford and I spent a delightful day with him. His wife is not less intelligent, even not a less ardent patriot than himself. He was, at the period I referred to, the first Manufacturer in Manchester, but was ruined in his business by the party spirit of the period. Felix Vaughan bequeathed him a property which had improved since so as to render him in his latter days an independent country gentleman."[3]

[1] Jerrold, pp. 115-16.                    [2] Jerrold, pp. 114.
[3] *Manchester Directory*, 1788, ed. Leary, 1870.

Thomas died on 2nd February, 1817, and was buried at St. Clement's Church, Chorlton-cum-Hardy, Lancashire. William Hone, the Radical publisher, wrote in appreciation of his steadfast faith and loyalty to their common cause: "The remains of Thomas Walker must not be consigned to the tomb without some tribute to his talents, his virtues and his sufferings.

"He was a steady and consistent friend both of civil and religious freedom. . . . His love of freedom, his hatred of tyranny, were not circumscribed within the narrow limits of his native land. Convinced that the natural tendency of liberty is to elevate the character and increase the happiness of man, he ardently wished to see its blessings extended all over the World."

Although this wish was not—and a hundred and fifty years later is still not—fulfilled, Walker died with a quiet mind; he had no reason for self-reproach, or remorse.

He himself might have written his epitaph, in the last words of the Preface to the *Review*:

"Were it possible that . . . the people of England should have wholly abandoned their national character and, conveying the poison of corruption to their own lips, should sit down tamely under an established despotism, those few who have endeavoured to prevent so deadly a calamity, will, at least, have the consolation, 'that as men employ the talents God has given them here, they shall accordingly receive their rewards at the close of the day, when their sun shall set, and when night shall put an end to their labours.'"

# BIBLIOGRAPHY

Sources include:

London Corresponding Society, Collected Papers.
Manchester Court Leet Records.
Reeves' Association, Collected Publications.
State Trials, 23, 24, 25.
Thomas Walker: *Review of some of the Political Events in Manchester*
(1794).
Verbatim Report of the Trial of Thomas Walker, 1794.
Verbatim Report of Walker's Libel Action, 1791.
Annual Register, 1790-1793.

*Unpublished Material:*

General Chamber of Manufacturers Papers (Assay Office,
Birmingham).
James Watt jr., Correspondence (Bristol).
Manchester Loyal Association Minute Book (Chetham
Library).
Manchester Reference Library Collection of Broadsheets,
1790-1794.
Privy Council Papers, 1793-1794.
Treasury Solicitor's Papers, 3495-3505 (Public Record Office).
Walker-Boulton-Watt Correspondence (Birmingham Central
Library).
Walker-Wedgwood Correspondence (Barlaston).

*Newspapers and Directories:*

*Manchester Directory*, 1788 to 1794, and 1788, ed. Leary (1870).
The *Manchester Herald*, the *Manchester Chronicle*, the *Manchester
Mercury* (1784-1795).

*Reference Books:*

Bowden, Witt: *Industrial Society in England towards the end of the
18th Century.*
Brockbank, W.: *Portrait of a Hospital.*

Brown, Philip: *The French Revolution in English History*.

Cestre, C.: *John Thelwall*.

Cole, G. D. H.: *Persons and Periods*.

Collins, Henry: "The London Corresponding Society" (*Democracy and the Labour Movement*).

Drinkwater, John: *Charles James Fox*.

Hardy, Thomas: *Memoir*.

Hone, William: *Memoir of Thomas Walker*.

Jerrold, Blanchard: "Biographical Sketch of Thomas Walker" (Preface of *The Original*, 1874).

Malone, Dumas: *The Public Life of Thomas Cooper*.

Redford, A.: *A History of Local Government in Manchester*.

Rose, J. Holland: *Pitt and Napoleon*.

Rosebery, Lord: *William Pitt the younger*.

Smith, E.: *The English Jacobins*.

Veitch, G. S.: *The Genesis of Parliamentary Reform*.

Webb, S. and B.: *Parish and County*.